To four women in ministry who have been mentors,
door openers, and friends:

Betty Coble Lawther
Pat Clary
Gerry Wakeland
Edna Myers

I thank God for you.

Contents

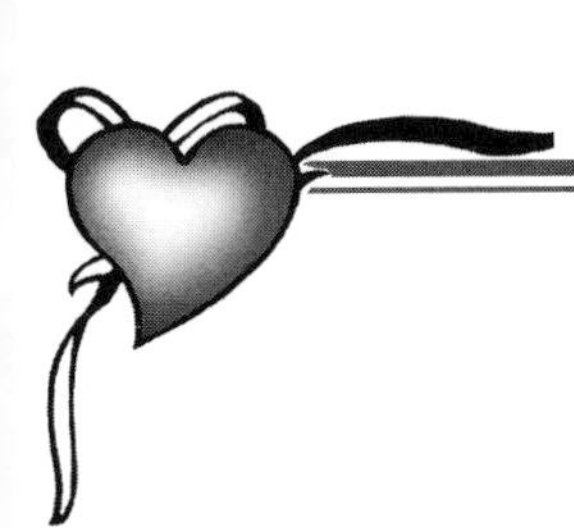

Introduction

Just about everyone loves the Book of the Psalms. In those poetic, heartfelt writings, the Psalmists pour out their hearts, seeking God's help and comfort in difficult times, but also praising the awesome Lord who is worthy to be exalted. Within the pages of the book you're holding, you will find stories about others' faith, lesson tips, and journal exercises that will gently guide you to express what is in your heart. You may seek God's help and comfort and also praise God for his awesomeness.

An Expressive Heart will inspire you as you discover a wealth of heartwarming devotional stories from those authors you're familiar with and those that you have yet to enjoy. The inspirational quote and reflection ideas for journaling will draw your heart to God in a new and fresh way.

I hope this book will become a favorite. It won't be just someone else's ideas or thoughts; it will contain yours also! Feel free to record the ways God is speaking to you and working in your life. As you seek His will or ponder His ways, you'll be drawn closer to your loving Master than ever before.

Be sure to date each of your entries, for your written thoughts will become a history of your journey with God. You'll find here seventy-two opportunities for making those important observations: twelve weeks of six days each week.

I trust this will make your time with God even more precious and meaningful. That is my desire and prayer for you.

—Kathy Collard Miller

Week One

Fast Facts About The Psalms

David Sanford

Blessed is the man who does not walk in the counsel of the wicked or stand in the way of sinners or sit in the seat of mockers. But his delight is in the law of the LORD, and on his law he meditates day and night.
Psalm 1:1–2

The book of Psalms is a treasure chest of valued gems of God's guidelines and instructions for godly living. Here are some fascinating facts about this popular and beloved book of the Bible.

The longest book in the Bible is Psalms.

The middle chapter in the Bible is Psalm 117. All of two verses, it's also the shortest chapter in Scripture.

The middle verse in the Bible is Psalm 118:8.

The longest chapter in the Bible is Psalm 119, an eight-fold acrostic 176 verses long.

The most memorized, quoted, and beloved chapter in the Bible is Psalm 23.

David wrote at least 75 psalms.

In addition to David, at least six other authors contributed to the book of Psalms.

Psalm 88 is the only psalm that ends without some sense of praise or hope in God.

The key word in the Psalms, "praise," appears 211 times, compared with 129 occurrences in all the rest of Scripture combined.

Hebrew poetry "rhymes" ideas—the first line makes a statement and the next line repeats, expands, or contrasts that idea. This unique parallel poetic structure translates especially well into other languages.

Psalms 25, 34, 37, 111, 112, 119, and 145 are examples of acrostic Hebrew poetry. In these seven psalms, the first letter of each line, verse, or stanza begins with a successive letter of the Hebrew alphabet. Their acrostic nature isn't readily apparent in English translations.

Psalms 25 and 34 are twin acrostics. Both duplicate and omit the same letters in their alphabetic pattern, both are written by David, and both conclude with words about God's redemption of Israel.

❤ *Lesson* ❤

The Psalms focus our hearts on the Lord in the unique way of worship, calling upon Him to deliver and bless. But most importantly, the poetry and prose of the Psalms exhorts us to review what our wonderful God has done in the past and to rehearse His wonderful attributes.

The attitude with which we should read the Psalms is included in the word "selah," which appears seventy-one times throughout the Psalms. Commentators believe it has the idea of "Pause here!" Reading the Psalms with a worshipful spirit will help us to pause and consider the greatness of our mighty God. And when we do that, as the Psalmist declares in the first Psalm, we will lead godly lives and delight in focusing on God's "love letter" to us—the Scriptures.

The Psalms are "an anatomy of all the parts of the soul" since "there is not an emotion of which any one can be conscious that it is not here represented as in a mirror."
—John Calvin

❤ Journal Exercise ❤

What do you like best about the Psalms? How do they minister to you? Can you think of a time that God used a Psalm in a powerful way to inspire, delight, or comfort you? Maybe a portion even pulled you up out of a pit of despair or hopelessness. What do you hope to gain from using this book and worshiping God through it? —KCM

Rooted In The Right Place

Tim Thomas

He is like a tree planted by streams of water, which yields its fruit in season and whose leaf does not wither. Whatever he does prospers.
Psalm 1:3

Once, on a fishing trip in the mountains of northern Georgia, I noticed a small tree growing out of a rock in the middle of the river. Many years ago, a wayward seed must have somehow drifted into a tiny crack in the boulder. There, nourished by the soil and nutrients that had also collected in the little rift, the tree sprang up.

We fished far beyond the little tree that day, but I could not forget the sight. When it first sprang forth, the seedling probably looked much like any other. No doubt, it experienced tremendous growth during its first years.

But I was struck by the thought that the little tree would probably never get any larger than when I saw it. It bore no fruit, and its few leaves looked tired and frail. The crack in the rock could hold only so much soil, so the tree's roots would have to make do in scanty, infertile ground. It might never produce any fruit, and the first strong flood would likely sweep it away.

❤ *Lesson* ❤

Many Christians are like that little tree. Upon their glorious awakening to Christ's grace, they spring forth almost instantly, seeming to grow by leaps and bounds. The excitement and freshness of their new life bursts forth and shows itself to all around. But if they aren't careful, new believers can miss the foundation that brings stability and growth during the trials of life. When Satan buffets, or when God allows difficulty to improve their character, the unstable believer can easily lose hope and give up. Those first times of suffering after conversion can be very confusing and disheartening to those who are new to the Christian walk.

New believers need to learn the many principles that are taught in God's Word in order to continue growing strong. Without the firm foundation of His Word written on our hearts, we can never become as fruitful as the Father desires. Only through total dependence on Him and His promises can we stand in the stormy times and successfully reach those who don't know Him. Then we'll be like the tree of Psalm 1:3.

Along the riverbank, just a few feet away from that little tree, were towering hemlocks and oaks, and beautiful, flowering rhododendron. They stand in good soil, and their roots intertwine underground for untold distances. Even in the worst of storms, most of these giants will not be moved. Year in and year out, they bring forth good fruit in abundance. When those huge trees are gone, others will take their place, a testimony to the fruitful predecessors.

As believers in Christ, we need to dig our roots deeply into the good soil of His Word. We should hide His words in our hearts, committing His precious instructions to memory. They should be the foundation of our faith, and the direction of our growth. Only in this way can we be sure to stand firm in our belief, bringing forth fruit in His name and His time, prospering in our efforts—like a tree planted by streams of water.

"Neglect of the Word is the explanation of the small fruitage of many a life."
—R. A. Torrey

❤ Journal Exercise ❤

Do you see yourself as the Psalmist's secure and fruitful tree or as the little tree in the crevice? How have you arrived at either one? What has contributed to your position? What kind of tree does God want you to be? Describe your life if you were that secure and fruitful tree. What does God want you to do in His power in order to become that kind of tree? —KCM

When I Consider Thy Heavens

Stuart Briscoe

When I consider your heavens, the work of your fingers, the moon and the stars, which you have set in place, what is man that you are mindful of him, the son of man that you care for him?
Psalm 8:3–4

All through history man has gazed at the heavens. Sometimes he has gotten into trouble, as Galileo did. Other times he has derived great insight, as the Magi did.

In recent days, however, man has set his sights on the heavens in a new way. With consummate skill and courage, he has begun exploring the heavens. He has accepted the challenge of space. Politically, scientifically, economically, and occasionally spiritually he has explored the heavens that have enthralled him so long.

The first American astronaut came back believing in God more than when he took off. Ironically, the first Russian cosmonaut returned more convinced of the nonexistence of God than when he left. The reverent soul of the astronaut saw order and beauty and attributed both to an orderly, beautiful God. The cosmonaut didn't expect to find God up there and was neither surprised nor disappointed that he didn't see Him.

Both men, of course, were acting on presuppositions. But one of those presuppositions is wrong. It must be said that if the believer in God is wrong he has lost nothing, but if the unbeliever is wrong, he has lost everything!

❤ Lesson ❤

When the Psalmist looked at the heavens, he didn't do so to bolster his presuppositions; he was moved to questions. His reverent soul humbly asked, "When I consider Thy heavens . . . what is man that Thou art mindful of him?"

I like this approach to the "What is man?" question. It has content and humility and approaches the problem of man with a deep sense of wonder and reverence. The question is asked in context of the universe as a whole and the Creator as the One who has the answer.

When the great philosophical question is asked this way, it can be answered. Asked any other way, it will never be answered.

Despite all the harsh attacks that have been made on the biblical view of man, it must be stated quite firmly that nowhere else is such a high view of man taught. From no other source will man ever gain the impression that he is anything more than a puzzle living in the middle of a muddle. But the Bible declares that man is the intelligent product of an intelligent Creator.

"Man without God is a seed upon the wind."
—Unknown

❤ Journal Exercise ❤

We are beings created by the same God who called into existence the awesome heavens. Do such musings make you feel small in comparison, or important because God created you too!? What have you gained as a result of believing in that kind of awesome God? What do you think unbelievers are deprived of by not believing? If you don't believe in God, why not? —KCM

A Lesson From The Tax Man

Lloyd John Ogilvie

Though you probe my heart and examine me at night, though you test me, you will find nothing; I have resolved that my mouth will not sin.
Psalm 17:3

A friend of mine was called by his tax consultant and told that the IRS had questioned his income tax return and had made an additional charge. Without investigating the reason he said, "Pay it! Pay it." He assumed he was wrong, when all the IRS wanted was an explanation.

But the tax consultant was a wise man and a good friend. He said, "Sounds like some old fears have reared their ugly head. Don't assume you've made a mistake until we are sure you have!"

The same thing could be said about so much of our reaction to criticism. The Lord helps us deal with past failures so we can be honest with ourselves in the present. What a comfort! We can own our true guilt and be forgiven, and we can disown false guilt and live with assurance.

The source of lasting integrity is God alone. David experienced the comfort of that. He went inward to the living center of his soul to investigate the possibility of wrong. He found no just reason for the accusations. He was not defensive but honestly analytical. Self-vindication was not enough; he had to experience the exoneration of the Lord. We need that exoneration, too, when general guilt feelings become so pervasive that we feel guilty every time we are criticized. The Lord wants to set us free from that syndrome. Only His grace can release us from that kind of soul malady.

❤ Lesson ❤

It's taken me a long time to learn that everything isn't my fault, just as John Ogilvie writes. God knows my heart inside and out. He knows the truth. If He says I'm not at fault then I don't have to feel guilty.

When you next feel guilty, ask God the truth. Let Him be the judge. Regardless of what other people think or say, refuse to let guilty feelings and thoughts make you feel bad—if God doesn't indicate it. You'll be set free. —KCM

"The avoidance of one small fib . . . may be a stronger confession of faith than a whole 'Christian philosophy' championed in lengthy, forceful discussion."
—Helmut Thielicke

❤ Journal Exercise ❤

Some of us just feel guilty all the time! And there are others whom we wish would feel guilty more often! Which one of those are you most of the time? What would other people say about your level of uprightness? How do you feel when your honesty is questioned? What does your response say about whose approval you most need: others' or God's? How do you want to react the next time someone questions your honor? —KCM

The Encourager

DiAnn Mills

He brought me out into a spacious place; he rescued me because he delighted in me.
Psalm 18:19

As a child, I lived on a small farm in central Ohio. Among our assortment of pets, my sister, brother, and I had a white spotted pony named Tony and a collie-and-shepherd mix dog named Laddie. The two animals were constant companions, and I felt certain they talked to each other. Laddie would bark and Tony would nod and paw the ground. As friends go, they were the best.

One spring, a flood washed out many of the rural roads and kept us all inside. As I gazed out over a steep hill to a creek that wound its way around the farm, I saw Tony trapped by rising water on the opposite side. My heart sank, and panic paralyzed me. Not far from where the pony stood, a fence separated our land from the adjoining farm. I feared the pony might be pushed against the fence and drown in the rapidly rising water.

Then I saw Laddie race across the field and down the hill to the swelling creek. I pressed my nose up against the window, holding my breath so as not to cloud my view. He barked repeatedly, but the pony did not move. After a few moments, Laddie jumped in and swam across to his friend. Once by Tony's side, he began barking again. He'd hurry to the water's edge and then back to the pony to encourage him on, but Tony's feet stayed firmly rooted on dry ground. Repeatedly Laddie coaxed the pony, but nothing happened.

Finally Laddie approached Tony and they nuzzled together. To me it looked like a kiss, a whisper, and a word of love. This time Laddie took a step and Tony took one too. Slowly the two moved into the rushing water. They waded in the muddy swirling mass until the dog started swimming and the pony joined him. I remember laughing and crying at the same time as the two emerged safely on the bank. Barking happily, Laddie ran circles around his friend, congratulating Tony on an excellent job. Like two children at play, they sped back to the shelter and warmth of the barn.

Lesson

As an adult, that sweet scene has served to remind me many times how God delivers us from the depths of despair.

How difficult it is to place our faith and trust in Him when the world's woes threaten to drown us. Yet God is right there offering encouragement and love when we want to simply drown. How precious to experience the joy of taking one more step into treacherous waters with our Lord and reaching the other side safely.

The Psalmist assures us that God does want to bring us to a safe and spacious place. Why? Because He delights in us!

"Behind the dim unknown standeth God within the shadows keeping watch above His own."
—James Russell Lowell

❤ Journal Exercise ❤

When we're drowning in life's cares, we can't even see the place of safety, yet our heavenly Father does. What obstacle seems overwhelming to you today? What do you think your Father God sees on the other side? What step of faith into the water of uncertainty does He want you to take, knowing He will "swim" beside you until you arrive at a spacious place of safety? —KCM

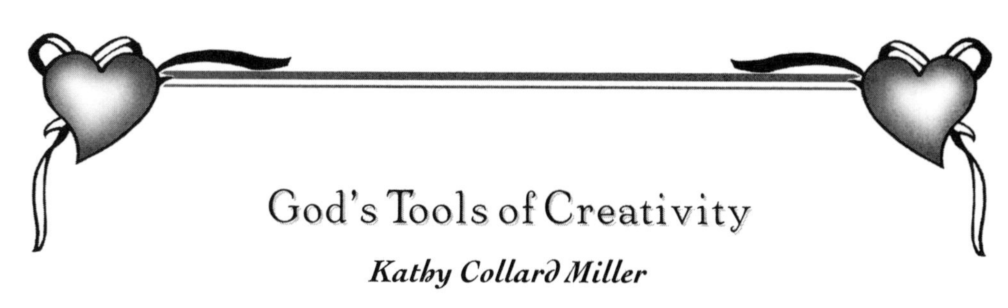

God's Tools of Creativity

Kathy Collard Miller

He is the God who avenges me, who subdues nations under me, who saves me from my enemies. You exalted me above my foes; from violent men you rescued me.
Psalm 18:47–48

A friend painted a small canvas for me showing a sailboat leaving a harbor and sailing out to sea. I propped up the painting in my living room, and as I viewed it from a distance, it was beautiful. When I moved up closer to admire it, I noticed a brushstroke of green that didn't quite fit. From that viewpoint I saw other colors that didn't seem to blend well. *That's strange,* I thought. When I moved back from the picture, the "flaws" disappeared. *What seem to be mistakes blend together to make a lovely picture.*

Later that day, I looked through my journal from several years before and read of the fears, worries, and traumas that I was struggling with at that time. Our son, Mark, was suffering from continual ear infections, and we were considering having tubes put in his ears. The teacher for our daughter, Darcy, was hinting that it might be a good idea for her to be kept back a grade in school.

The passage of time allowed me to stand back from those circumstances and see God's creative touch. I didn't know what God was going to do at the time, but now I can see how He worked. God blended those situations into a beautiful picture, developing my growth and trust in the Lord. Mark's ears healed without surgery. Darcy moved ahead in school and is now a college graduate.

❤ *Lesson* ❤

You and I face overwhelming circumstances as our "foes." We usually don't have enemies ready to kill us like King David wrote about in his songs, but we face situations that could cause us to lose our trust and faith in God. Yet, God is continually and lovingly wielding His brush upon the canvas of our lives. In difficult times, we only see the yellow glob of grief, the blue streak of illness, and the green smudge of confusion. When we stand back and see God's hand over time, we can rejoice in His protection from our "foes."

The next time God's creativity seems to go haywire in the circumstances He allows in your life, be assured He knows what He's doing on the canvas of your life. How He defeats the enemies of your life will turn into something beautiful as you cooperate with Him. The different colors will blend together to create beauty and strength.

"As in nature, as in art, so in grace; it is rough treatment that gives souls, as well as stones, their lustre. The more the diamond is cut the brighter it sparkles; and in what seems hard dealing, there God has no end in view but to perfect His people."
—Thomas Guthrie

❤ Journal Exercise ❤

What "globs" of paint is God putting on the canvas of your life? Review any journals you have from the past, or reflect upon how God has taken past problems and turned them into the beautiful canvas of your life. —KCM

WEEK TWO

Laura DuBell Drewer

Keep your servant also from willful sins; may they not rule over me . . . May the words of my mouth and the meditation of my heart be pleasing in your sight, O LORD, my Rock and my Redeemer.
Psalm 19:13a–14

During my lifetime, I have heard many jokes that I cannot remember. However, there is one joke I heard as a teenager that I wish I could forget. When I heard it, I was very impressionable and it was very graphic to all my senses. It invaded my thoughts, my emotions, and my heart and embedded its roots deep in my mind.

Down through the years, at the strangest times, in the most unusual circumstances, that joke kept coming to my mind. What a battle for me not to rehearse its every detail in my mind. It was so easy to meditate on it, fantasize the experience, and embrace the feelings.

Finally, while reading Psalm 19:14, I experienced victory. I realized I had a choice to entertain thoughts, as a cow chewing its cud, or to dismiss them from my mind.

I remembered the biblical story of the woman whose home was possessed by a demon. When the evil spirit had been driven out, the unoccupied house was swept clean and put in order. Then the evil spirit brought in seven other spirits more wicked than itself to live there.

I realized that it is not enough to clean my mind of filth, but I needed to fill that emptiness with something clean, refreshing, and inspiring. When I ask, God gives me the power to "think on things that are true, honest, just, pure, lovely, and of good report."

Desperately, I prayed, "Lord, please give me a substitute for those thoughts."

The words of a beautiful hymn by William Featherstone flooded my mind, "My Jesus, I love thee. I know thou art mine. For thee all the follies of sin I resign." I claimed those words as a wonderful gift from God.

Now, whenever that joke (because it is still imbedded in my memory) or any other thought I do not want to entertain invades my mind, I switch over to "My Jesus, I love thee."

❤ Lesson ❤

In Psalm 19, David praises God for His creation which daily declares the glory of God. He acknowledges that it is God's Word that warns him of potential evil and he realizes that there is great reward in keeping it. Then he prays that God will be glorified by the words of his mouth and the meditation of his heart. In addressing God as his Lord, his Rock and his Redeemer, he rests, confident that God will answer his prayer.

You and I can set a guard at our mind's door—a filter through which everything desiring admittance must be strained. When unwelcome thoughts plague you, praise God by rehearsing His great attributes in a song or verse of Scripture. You'll find that deliberately focusing on the Lord leaves little room for anything displeasing to Him.

"You are not what you think you are, but what you think, you are."
—Unknown

❤ Journal Exercise ❤

What unacceptable thoughts seem to "rule" over you most often? Make a list of ways to meditate on that which pleases God. Which would be most effective against the unacceptable thoughts that haunt you? Describe for God how intent you are on making your thoughts and words pleasing to Him. —KCM

A 3:00 A.M. Encounter

Maria Conklin

May the LORD answer you when you are in distress; may the name of the God of Jacob protect you.
Psalm 20:1

It was nearly 3:00 A.M. by the time I got off work. Usually I was finished by midnight, but Saturdays were my nights to help close the restaurant. I worked nights as a waitress on Manhattan's East Side. Days I spent at auditions, dance classes, voice lessons, and acting workshops. I longed to be in theater.

The bus departed while I was still two blocks away, and the next one wasn't due for forty-five minutes. The walk across town to where my husband and I lived took only half an hour. Reluctantly, I started walking. Except for the taxis and an occasional prostitute, the streets were deserted.

I walked quickly, eager to get home but enjoying the time alone. As I walked, I talked to the Lord. I told Him about my day and asked Him to keep me safe. As I often did while walking alone, I pretended I was walking hand in hand with Jesus. I knew that if Jesus was with me, nothing could happen to me that He did not allow.

As I got to Columbus Circle I relaxed, knowing I had only seven more blocks to go. This was my neighborhood, and I knew just about every crack in the sidewalk.

Then, out of the corner of my eye, I noticed him. He was carrying a liquor bottle in one hand and was obviously drunk. He was looking directly at me. He headed right toward me, and I could tell he was agitated.

My heart thumped. My face flushed a sudden red. I knew there was no one within shouting distance.

I told myself I wasn't alone. "Jesus be with me," I prayed, mentally clasping His hand with my left hand a little more firmly as though He were physically with me.

The drunken man stopped. He looked first at me, then over my left shoulder with fear. He backed away, continuing to stare at the place beside me.

As I continued my walk towards home, I was thankful for the Lord's presence in my life.

When I am afraid, I try to remember that God is trustworthy and He is my protector. I can't always count on other people to be there for me, but I can always count on Jesus. With Jesus beside me I can let go of my fears.

Sometimes when I think about what happened that night, I wonder what would have happened had I not been conscious of the fact that Jesus was walking beside me. I will never know. But I know that Jesus is always with me. No matter where I am. No matter what the circumstances.

The Psalmist knew the truth of God's protection; do you?

"When I am finally able to accept my Father's perfect love for me, then my fears can relax. I know that He will not allow anything to enter my life without first giving it permission. And I know that He will not permit anything to enter my life without also providing His presence."
—Don Baker

❤ Journal Exercise ❤

Knowing God is protecting us doesn't guarantee we won't experience bad things. What does it mean to you to know God is protecting you? What is your greatest fear that signifies it's difficult for you to believe God will watch over you? What does that say about your opinion of God and His power? If you have a strong sense of God's protection, what would you say to someone who is fearful? —KCM

Becoming A Person Who Dares

Ileana Landon

**They are brought to their knees and fall,
but we rise up and stand firm.
Psalm 20:8**

A few years back, a very special friend gave me a postcard book called *Women Who Dared*. The book features some of the world's most prominent women of all time—women like Rosa Parks, the black American civil rights activist who sparked a successful bus boycott in 1955–56 when she refused a bus driver's order to give her seat to a white man. Parks dared to do something no other black woman had done before.

Also included is Eleanor Roosevelt. The wife of a well-respected U.S. president, Mrs. Roosevelt was pivotal in the drafting and securing of the Universal Declaration of Human Rights.

The book features thirty other daring women from recent history. As I read about these women, I wondered, "God, how can I possibly become a woman who dares? What can I do to make this world a better place? How can I be more like these women? I'm not the wife of a president nor am I a woman who defies the status quo on a daily basis."

God gently reminded me that I dare to do risky things every day, yet I don't recognize them as daring. I may make the world only slightly better by impacting others with my witness for Christ, but I, too, dare. I dare to do the little things that add up to great things.

We dare to dream and sometimes even to act on those dreams. We dare to experiment with an entirely new recipe that fuels our

family and our souls. We dare to bring out our creativity through the nurturing of a garden or an infant. We dare to take on a challenging task at work when all we want to do is go to lunch. We even dare when we read a bedtime story to our toddler when we don't think we have the energy.

Perhaps you're like a friend of mine from church who is daring by starting a Moms In Touch chapter at her children's school so she and other mothers can pray for the children and school. You may have dared to be nice to someone this morning who wasn't nice to you last week. Or, you might be starting a company from your home because you want to see your children more often and want to make a difference in their lives.

Every day, we have an opportunity to dare. Every day God grants us a fresh, new morning to begin that project we want to finish. Every day we have a choice. The Psalmist encourages us to "stand firm." Today, we must promise ourselves and God that we will dare to be different—and rise up to represent Him. Dare to march to the beat of a different drum. Dare to help someone in need. Dare to open up that dusty Bible. Dare to take on an opportunity that will enable you to make a positive change in your life or the lives of others. Dare to make that phone call you've been putting off.

Today, we must dare to forgive and more importantly, dare to love. By doing these things and acknowledging them, perhaps, just perhaps, we'll make a greater difference and dare to do more. It's time to become a woman who dares.

"So many women just don't know how great they really are. They come to us all vogue outside and vague on the inside."

—Mary Kay Ash

❤ Journal Exercise ❤

What can you identify that you've done in the past that was daring? What is God calling you to do right now that requires you to "rise up and stand firm?" Journal about how you anticipate you'll feel after it's done. Then give God the glory for the work He does through you. —KCM

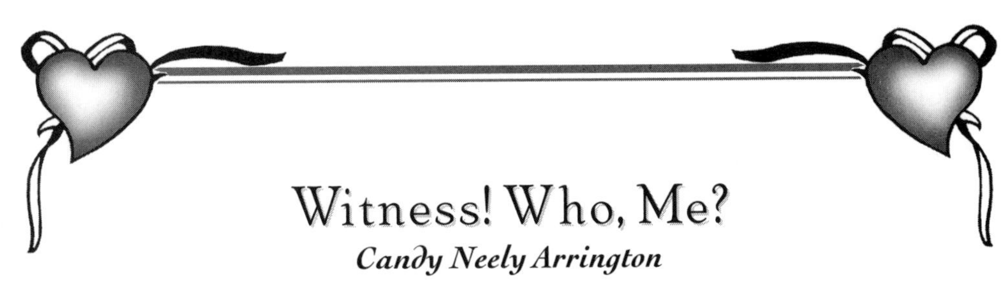

Witness! Who, Me?

Candy Neely Arrington

But you, O LORD, be not far off; O my Strength, come quickly to help me.
Psalm 22:19

I saw him coming toward me. I watched him discreetly from behind my sunglasses. He had been sitting on a lounge chair, drink in hand, but now was staggering across the sand toward me.

"Great," I thought, "just what I need—a drunk at 6:30 A.M. on an otherwise deserted beach."

I quickened my pace and pretended not to notice his rapid approach but it was no use. He fell into step beside me asking the time. "Lord, help!" I breathed a silent prayer.

My companion's inebriation made him talkative and as we walked on, he poured out his story. His life was one of pain and disappointment—a broken marriage, lost jobs, struggles and failures, and all the pleasures he had indulged in to ease the pain. I listened and prayed. At some point, I mustered up the courage to ask him, with shaking voice, if God had ever been a part of his life. This was difficult for me because I had been raised to believe that I should witness by my example—not by my words. Since I couldn't live my faith before him, if he was going to hear the message, I was going to have to speak it.

Fear gripped me. "Lord, don't ask me to do this. I can't. I'll mess it up," I argued with God. His still, small voice replied, "Trust my Spirit living within you."

Feeling more bold, I told this man about Jesus and what He meant in my life. The man was a skeptic and assured me that "religion" wasn't the answer for him.

As we neared the end of our journey, I saw two deserted chairs on the beach. The Holy Spirit clearly said, "Sit him down and lead him through John 3:16 by substituting his name for the word 'world' and then through the sinner's prayer." I obeyed. There, on a beach just beginning to show signs of activity, Paul prayed and asked Jesus into his heart and life.

The man I had tried to escape an hour before turned and waved as he walked away. I've never seen him again. I don't know how his life has been lived since then, but I know that God used me, his reluctant servant, to draw a hurting soul to Himself.

❤ Lesson ❤

That day on the beach showed me that I could step out of my comfort zone and trust the Holy Spirit to guide and guard me through an unusual experience. All God asked of me that day was to trust him to give me the courage to share the gospel. I was not an eloquent evangelist; I was God's reluctant servant.

The experience also taught me that if I could witness to a total stranger, I could surely invite an unbelieving neighbor into my home and share the gospel over a cup of coffee. In all the ways that the Lord challenges us to share Him with others, He promises to provide the strength that the Psalmist asked for and that we need. God provides it through His Holy Spirit's presence as Psalm 22:19 indicates.

Sharing your faith doesn't require a divinity degree. It only requires an obedient servant empowered by the Holy Spirit dwelling within.

"For courage mounteth with occasion."
—William Shakespeare

❤ Journal Exercise ❤

What causes your fear or hesitation most often? When you worked through that hesitation, how did God strengthen you and what happened? Is there anyone that God is asking you to reach out to now? What do you plan to do about it? If you easily speak of God to others, to what do you credit that? How could you share that ability with others who are fearful? —KCM

I'll Be At The End Of The Pier!

Judy Gale

He makes me lie down in green pastures, he leads me beside quiet waters, he restores my soul. He guides me in paths of righteousness for his name's sake.
Psalm 23:2–3

"I'll be at the end of the pier!"

The rush and bustle of the day had finally gotten to me, and I didn't care who heard me. The family looked at me curiously and sighed. I headed for my favorite chair with my Bible.

What is so tremendously absurd about this scene is that we don't live near water! We live in town, next to the library, and a big parking lot. There isn't a lake, river, or even a pond in sight. A filled bathtub is the nearest body of water in our entire neighborhood!

The day had started pleasantly. The sun was shining, the lunch boxes were all packed, the car was filled with gas, the laundry was folded and put away. Yet I knew something was not quite right. What was it? I hurriedly drove the kids to school. Then, off to a meeting at the library for the summer reading program.

Something still was not quite right. What was it?

After the meeting, I took my crumpled grocery list out of my coat pocket and rushed through the store. The next stop was the Ladies Luncheon at church. Rushing past the ticket chairman at the last minute, I greeted the pastor's wife. She appeared so together and calm, it really bothered me. Especially today.

Why? Something still was not quite right. What was it?

During the slide presentation following the luncheon, the Lord told me exactly what was wrong. I had missed my time with Him that morning. I had allowed the whole world to edge in and take away that special time. That peaceful, still time with Him prepared me for each day. It reminded me of being at the lake when I was a child. Sitting at the end of the pier dangling my feet into the quiet water made me feel everything was right and in order. I was happy at the end of the pier.

❤ Lesson ❤

Spending time with Him is one of the simplest and most refreshing pleasures in my life. I treasure the time I am in the presence of God. It's my "cure-all" for the daily delirium called life. That time can happen anywhere I am with my Bible. His presence is with me continually. I can be in my favorite chair or sitting on the patio at sunrise. Or, I can be right in the middle of a hectic schedule and an unfinished list of errands.

Sometimes, it amazes me that my "pier" time is so refreshing and renewing. His words to me are a time of restoration, as the Psalmist says. It's there I realize I am being washed by the water of the Word and the "end of the pier" becomes a reality to my heart. God leads me into stillness where my soul finds rest. As the Psalmist describes it, He wants to guide me to green pastures of knowing He's in loving control. He wants to lead me in actions of righteousness that bring peace because I have no guilty conscience.

So, when life gets busy, you'll find me "at the end of the pier." When was the last time you headed for the pier?

"Not till we have lost the world do we begin to find ourselves."
—Henry David Thoreau

❤ Journal Exercise ❤

What do you like best about your private time with God? Journal a note of thanks to Him for it. What's the biggest obstacle to finding that time with Him? Tell Him how choosing something else makes you feel. Now journal how you think God feels when you miss spending undivided time with Him. What new strategy will you make for keeping your appointment with God more often? —KCM

What Are You Haunted By?

Oswald Chambers

Who, then, is the man that fears the LORD? He will instruct him in the way chosen for him.
Psalm 25:12

What are you haunted by? You may say—by nothing, but we are all haunted by something, generally by ourselves, or, if we are Christians, by our experience. The Psalmist says we are to be haunted by God. The abiding consciousness of the life is to be God, not thinking about Him. The whole of our life inside and out is to be absolutely haunted by the presence of God. A child's consciousness is so mother-haunted that although the child is not consciously thinking of its mother, yet when calamity arises, the relationship that abides is that of the mother. So we are to live and move and have our being in God, to look at everything in relation to God, because the abiding consciousness of God pushes itself to the front all the time.

If we are haunted by God, nothing else can get in, no cares, no tribulation, no anxieties. We see now why our Lord so emphasized the sin of worry. How can we dare be so utterly unbelieving when God is round about us? To be haunted by God is to have an effective barricade against all the onslaughts of the enemy.

"His soul shall dwell at ease." In tribulation, misunderstanding, slander, in the midst of all these things, if our life is hid with Christ in God, He will keep us at ease.

Oswald Chambers refers to us being "haunted" by the Lord. That's a wonderful way to describe the "fear" that the Psalmist

refers to in Psalm 25:12. Being haunted is the idea that we are constantly aware of God's availability and invitation to take hold of His power. That's a kind of fear, or awe, because we are recognizing how great God is and how much we need Him.

You and I can turn our attention to our wonderful God moment by moment. Stress, anger, confusion, and discontentment will diminish as we do, because we're allowing our trust in God to defuse their hold over us. That's allowing Him to "haunt" us! —KCM

"Worry is interest paid on trouble before it becomes due."
—William R. Inge

❤ Journal Exercise ❤

Various worries and negative ideas can consume our thoughts. But God wants our minds to be filled with thoughts of Him. Does that sound exciting or burdensome? Tell God why. If your thoughts were constantly of Him, what difference would that make in your life? What one small change can you make that will help you think of Him more often? —KCM

Week Three

His Little Girl

Barbara Curtis

**Though my father and mother forsake me,
the LORD will receive me.
Psalm 27:10**

I remember the day my dad left. He hugged me and cried. The skimpy dress of a five-year-old girl couldn't protect me from the chill that gathered around my arms and legs. The scratchy, ticklish whiskers—would I feel them no longer? The arms that felt so safe—would they be gone forever? *What will it be like not to have a father?*

Shuffled with two brothers between foster home, relatives, and—when things worked out, my mother—I survived the tough times. My innocence gave way early on to a cynic's worldview: *Don't depend on anyone and no one will disappoint you.* Only when this unsustainable strategy failed me and I was more alone than ever, did I finally face my fatherlessness.

In my thirties, I sensed the void in my life was a spiritual one, and I launched a search for God. For someone like me, the New Age movement held enormous appeal. I could wander into nooks and crannies, borrowing this and that to construct an image of God to mesh with my own deficiencies. Crippled by the lack of a real father in my life, seeing God only as some remote and impersonal force, my hope was that through understanding, I could appropriate the force—recognizing the New Age "wisdom" of "God within me"—and then manipulate it to find happiness. With my eyes on the ground, happiness was as high as I could aim my sight. I never thought to seek God's love.

Amazingly, in the midst of my search, He remained faithful in loving me. No matter how much I wandered for seven more years, He patiently waited, protecting me from harm and drawing me nearer.

My husband helped to soften me. Watching him parent our children was like peeking through a frosted pane into a warm and cozy room within. Although seeing my children experience a happy childhood was the next best thing to having one myself, I longed sometimes to climb inside that room and receive that kind of love myself.

My husband's example of unconditional love prepared me for the moment I first heard God was my Father! Of course, I wanted a Father! Through my heavenly Father, I received the father I'd always wanted—and I will always be His little girl!

❤ Lesson ❤

Is it not a miracle that we who missed an earthly father's love can be healed to receive the love of our heavenly Father? The greatest privilege for each of us is to call him Abba, Father. According to Vine's Word Dictionary, "Abba is a word framed by the lips of infants and betokens unreasoning trust. Father expresses an intelligent apprehension of the relationship. The two together express the love and intelligent confidence of a child."

The Psalmist wrote that though our earthly parents disappoint us—even reject us— we can relax in the embrace of our heavenly Father. As His beloved child we can be trusting, dependent, and filled with faith in the arms that will never let us go.

"Dukes and lords are of no account; orphans take rank here."
—George Müller

❤ Journal Exercise ❤

What fond memory do you have of your parents' love? What hurtful experience did you suffer at a parent's hand? As you relive that incident, can you picture your heavenly Father's loving presence caring for you and protecting you from even greater harm? What was He saying to you as you experienced that hurt? What is He saying right now to you as your Abba Father? —KCM

Waiting, Waiting, Waiting...

Barbara Johnson

**Wait for the LORD; be strong and take heart
and wait for the LORD.
Psalm 27:14**

Here in Southern California, one of the places where we have to do a lot of waiting is in traffic jams. The only good thing about going nowhere on one of our multilane freeways is that it gives me a good excuse to let my mind wander. (Of course, it sometimes wanders off completely, leaving me sitting there wondering where it has gone—and wondering where I was going when I got started!)

Whenever I'm stuck in traffic or forced to do some waiting, I head off on a different path—mental path, that is. My favorite "mind trips" take me right up to heaven. I love thinking about what it will be like when the trumpet toots and we scoot out of here. Even though millions of us will be flying away to meet Jesus in the clouds, isn't it nice to think there will be no traffic jams in the sky, no lines to stand in, and no car problems to contend with? That thought gives us the endurance we need to cling to the *first* part of Psalm 27:14 while enduring the *second* part:

Be strong and take heart and wait for the Lord.

Someone pointed out that we're not the only ones who have to wait. God is also experienced at waiting. When we're struggling through problems here on earth, trying to cope with the trials that block our way home, He longingly waits for us to turn to Him. He watches our stories unfold and waits for us to acknowledge His plan for our lives. He counts our tears and waits for us to cry out to Him. God is there with us wherever we are on the road of life.

❤ *Lesson* ❤

As Barbara Johnson points out, waiting time can be useful and good. We could think about how much we love our spouse or children. Or how we're going to bless them with a huge hug and smile when we next see them. The more we think about treating others with love while we wait, the more our waiting time won't seem so frustrating. We'll actually arrive at our destination with joy, rather than a complaint. —KCM

"He that can have patience can have what he will."
—Benjamin Franklin

❤ Journal Exercise ❤

Although God is not bound by time, what do you think He is eager to see happen? Make a list. How do you fit in with His plans for the future? In the past, what important thing did you have to patiently wait for? What happened when your longing was fulfilled? Does remembering that help you to wait more patiently now? If so, in what way? —KCM

When An Answer To Prayer Is Delayed

Evelyn Christenson

My times are in your hands; deliver me from my enemies and from those who pursue me.
Psalm 31:15

I was absolutely devastated when our denomination's Foreign Mission Board's examining doctor decided that my husband's war-related ulcers would not allow him to serve where finding milk and cream could be a problem—the standard treatment for ulcers in those days [early 1950s]. At the next foreign missions commissioning service, I sobbed as all the others were sent off—except us. For several years, I avoided that part of our denomination's annual meeting, for I could not face the hurt and bitterness in my soul when God's call to India had seemed so definite.

Chris had been a World War II bomber pilot and, in a burning B17 plane over Germany, he had promised God that if He would bring him safely to neutral territory he would serve Him the rest of his life. He even instructed pilots in the early Missionary Aviation Fellowship program. Then at the end of the preparation years at college and seminary, together we had accepted God's call to foreign missions in Assam, India. Chris was to be the first flying evangelist in that country, and we were ecstatic.

However, being the secretary to our college president for four years hardly had prepared me for the mission field. Even the difficult war years, three miscarriages, and other family tragedies hardly had prepared me either. And certainly, a liberal arts college education hadn't done all that much. But nobody had seemed very concerned about what I would do once I [arrived in India]. So I was as excited and committed as any missionary candidate could be.

But God's door to India for us stayed tightly shut for thirty whole years. However, God's answer really was not "no" but just His, *"I have much preparing to do in you."* And the steps of preparation have been long and slow. But in 1982, Chris and I finally went to India.

As I was speaking for the first time in New Delhi, I was so choked up that I could hardly speak. Tears kept filling my eyes as I told the women of my devastating disappointment in 1952—and now my overwhelming joy thirty years later.

❤ Lesson ❤

Our omniscient God has reasons for His timing in fulfilling calls. I'm sure He knew I was not ready to go to India in 1952. But these thirty years have prepared me through eighteen years in my husband's pastorates, the "What Happens When Women Pray" experimenting, my books, tapes, and the privilege of personally training hundreds of thousands to pray in seminars in the United States, Canada, and overseas.

As we left for India, included in the Scripture our Jan gave us were these words about God's sovereign timing from Psalm 31:15, "My times are in thy hand."

In our impatience, we try to tell God when we want our prayers answered. But how good God is to control the timing of His answers to our prayers.

"Blessed is the man who finds out which way God is moving and then gets going in the same direction."
—Unknown

❤ Journal Exercise ❤

One of the most difficult situations is waiting for a promise of God to be fulfilled. When you have to wait, why is it difficult? If you're waiting right now, what is your heart's cry to God? Express it fully with all the emotion your heart is holding. Now listen for what God says to you and write it down. —KCM

"Not My Hands, Lord!"

Heather Collard

**I will extol the LORD at all times;
his praise will always be on my lips.
Psalm 34:1**

"Not my hands, Lord!" I pleaded. Pain crept from my shoulders to my fingers, sending a numbing, tingling feeling throughout my arms. Moments after saying a joyful good-bye to friends, I had fumbled for the keys to my Pontiac, only to watch them clink to the pavement. Kneeling, I tried to scoop up the keys with my now curved fingers.

"Lord!" I cried in mixed frustration and pain, "Please help me!"

Panicked thoughts raced through my mind as I stood beside my car, unable to open the door. *What's wrong with me? This has never happened before. Will I lose the use of my hands completely? I'm only twenty-three years old; my hands shouldn't be like this!*

Tears flooded my cheeks as I tried to push the fearful thoughts aside and focus on opening the car door.

Something inside me prompted me to praise God. I didn't feel like singing, but I began hesitantly, "I love you, Lord, and I lift my voice . . ." Sobs erupted from my throat, but I forced myself to continue, ". . . to worship You. Oh my soul, rejoice . . ."

As my tears dropped on the pavement, I knelt a third time, forcing my curled fingers to hold onto the keys. It worked! Though my hands were still gnarled, I drove home as I continued to lift my voice, singing my worship of God! I couldn't explain how I could thank and give glory to God, but I knew He deserved my praise for His goodness—even though I didn't know whether or not He would heal my hands. I was amazed at the strength that surged within me from my singing. It made me want to worship Him even more.

Since my experience, I discovered I have degenerative disk disease. I've had numerous opportunities to reflect on what it means to have a continual attitude of praise. Daily I am reminded of the choice I have either to praise God or to grumble about the physical pain in my hands. I may never experience total healing, but that doesn't mean God doesn't deserve my praise. He alone knows what is best for me, and in the midst of my pain, He has revealed how much He truly loves me through His patience when I lack trust in His sovereignty.

The Psalmist declared that he would extol God. Extol means to "speak well" of someone. We extol God as we concentrate on His wonderful attributes, such as His goodness. He is faithful both in the hard times and in the good times. His nature never changes, but it's up to us to make the choice to appreciate who He is in all His greatness.

"Circumstances may appear to wreck our lives and God's plans, but God is not helpless among the ruins. . . . He comes in and takes the calamity and uses it victoriously, working out his wonderful plan of love."
—Eric Liddle

❤ Journal Exercise ❤

What are we communicating when we praise God? Dependence on Him? Acknowledgment that He knows better than we do? Could that be why we don't want to praise Him—because we want to follow our own impulses rather than His direction? When you do choose to praise God, what happens to your heart, mind and spirit? Write down the one thing you appreciate most about God today. Tell Him why. —KCM

Behind The Backboard

Beverly Hamel

I sought the LORD, and he answered me;
he delivered me from all my fears.
Psalm 34:4

One day, my dad took me to the park across a busy street from my grandmother's house. To get to the park, we had to go under an overpass. Although the rush of cars overhead scared me, it was all right because Daddy was there holding my hand. He wouldn't let anything happen to me. *I'm his little girl,* I thought as I grasped his hand confidently.

When we arrived at the park, we played hide-and-seek. Dad let me hide first. I was so sure he couldn't see me behind the chain link fence, but somehow he did. *Nothing gets past him.*

Then Dad hid and I looked for him, but couldn't find him. *This park is so huge and there's that scary traffic. He'll never hear me calling him.* Tears welled up in my eyes.

Then I heard someone call my name. Turning toward the baseball diamond, I saw Dad pop out from behind the batter's backboard. He trotted over to me and gathered me into his arms. "I'm here. I wouldn't leave you."

❤ Lesson ❤

Our sinful natures have made life confusing, like that heavy traffic on the street. Our disobedience creates a "hide-and-seek" mentality between our heavenly Father and ourselves. We pray frantically, hoping we'll find God or that He'll find us. We look everywhere we can think of to spot Him, yet our fear that He won't accept us blocks our ability to receive His unconditional love.

Yet, He's as close as our heart. His love diligently seeks to fill us before we even complete our prayer. Psalm 34:4 promises that He's as near as seeking Him. We don't need to "perform" perfectly or pray in a certain way. He knows our hearts and longs to have our attention. Just as a good father never abandons his children when they get into trouble, our good heavenly Father watches His children carefully to guide them.

True, it's a confusing life. It only seems our Father God doesn't know where we are. But He knows we're hiding behind the chain link fence. We may feel as though we're hidden, but He sees us all along. And through Jesus, He trots over to us, calling our names, and gathers us into His arms, consoling us with, "I'm here, I didn't leave you."

"To have found God is not an end in itself, but a beginning."
—Franz Rosenzweig

❤ Journal Exercise ❤

Sometimes we don't want God to "find" us because we're ashamed of how we're living or of the choices we've made. What have you tried to hide from Him? Can you be honest now and know He's waiting for you to call to Him for forgiveness and cleansing? Write down what you believe He'll say when you see Him come out from behind the backboard and trot over to you.
—KCM

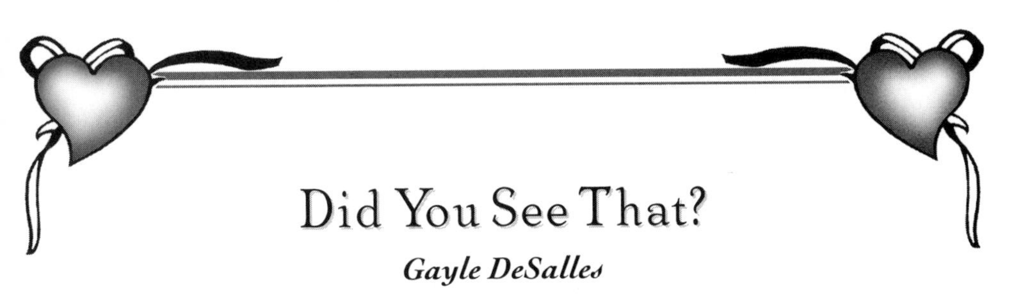

Did You See That?

Gayle DeSalles

O LORD, you have seen this; be not silent.
Do not be far from me, O LORD.
Psalm 35:22

I awoke to a sunny, crisp morning, a perfect day to take my friend's young son, Christopher, to the park. He squealed with delight as he caught his first glimpse of the swings. After he had "touched the sky," he walked over to a little boy playing in the sandbox. They immediately started playing together.

I looked on from a nearby bench, serenely celebrating their innocence. I cherished these moments when I could assume my role as "Auntie Gayle" to this precocious four-year-old. Eavesdropping, I heard the boys speak of good guys and bad guys and how they could protect the cowboys from the monsters.

Their merriment was disrupted when another boy approached. Slightly older than the two in the sandbox, he was rough and bossy. Christopher attempted to include the new boy, explaining to him the game they were playing. He gruffly brushed Christopher aside. Suddenly Christopher was the "odd man out." Dejected, Christopher looked up at me. His eyes revealed his bewilderment and hurt: "What just happened here?"

I nodded and smiled. He seemed to know I was saying, *Yes, I saw.*

I ached for Christopher. I wanted to march up to that bully and demand that he either be kind or leave. I wanted to pick Christopher up and comfort him. I did neither. This was Christopher's battle. Instead, I prayed, "God, protect Christopher's tender young heart."

Before long he'd had enough and walked over to me. I clasped his hand, and we walked back to the car. "I'm so proud of you, Christopher." I tried to explain to him what had happened, but he seemed to understand all too well. Christopher had a keen sense of what was right and fair, and this situation had not been fair at all.

❤ Lesson ❤

When Christopher looked up at me from his sandbox, he wasn't asking that I remedy the situation; he simply needed to know that I had seen how mean this boy had been. My nod and smile assured him I had.

I feel like Christopher sometimes. As a Christian, I aspire to be a godly example of Christ's love to individuals God places in my life. Sometimes, my world is disrupted by a curt remark, a harsh glance, or worse. I've meant no ill will, yet suddenly I'm thrust into the midst of conflict. Bewildered and hurt, I glance around. No one is there; no one sees. I'm left alone, bleeding.

But I am not alone. I do have a Witness—Jesus Christ Himself. Nothing escapes His notice as the Psalmist bears witness. When we are wounded, we must remember to look up into the face of our heavenly Father. He is standing close. If we'll "catch His eye," we'll see Him nodding in assurance, "Yes, Child, I saw that." In His infinitely great love and compassion, He will wrap His arms around us. Our sorrow will be no greater than we can endure. And as for those who have injured us, they will give an account to Him one day.

"With God in charge of our defenses, there will be peace within."
—T. T. Faichney

❤ Journal Exercise ❤

Being mistreated or misunderstood is very difficult to handle. If that has happened to you recently, journal your feelings and thoughts about it. Do you see Jesus nodding and smiling? What do you think He wants to do in your life by allowing this pain? Can you write a note of thanksgiving to Him—even for the hurt—because you can see the positive results He's bringing? —KCM

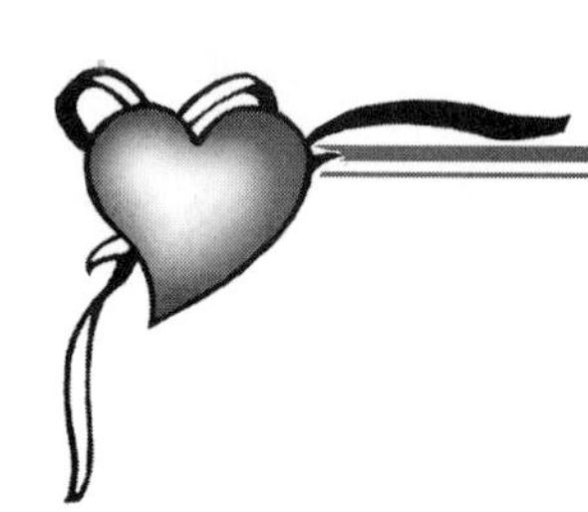

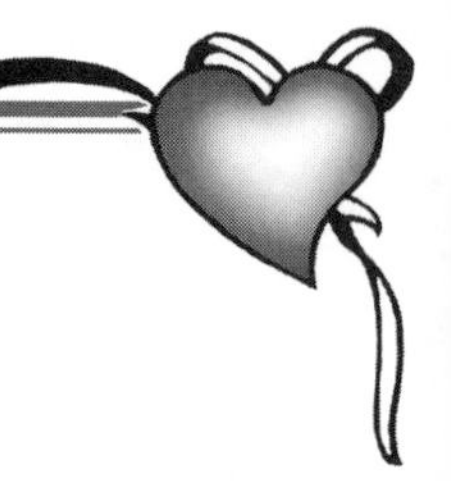

WEEK FOUR

Sheltered

Patsy Clairmont

How priceless is your unfailing love! Both high and low among men find refuge in the shadow of your wings.
Psalm 36:7

I love a porch that encircles a home like a warm hug. I love open porches that suggest availability, especially ones lined with inviting chairs that wordlessly invite passersby to sit a spell and catch their breaths. I love tiny porches that promise intimate chats and friendly secrets, and expansive porches that insist on peopled celebrations. I appreciate porches that beckon me out of the storm and into their safe covering. And ones so grand that people snap pictures from their cars as they cruise by.

I am a hopeless romantic when it comes to porches. I think every home should have at least one. Perhaps I long for bygone times when neighbors called from their porches to yours to see how your day fared. When even strangers were greeted as they sauntered by, and children were given peppermints as they jump-roped past your porch. When schedules weren't so hectic, leaving time for carefree chats and leisurely spells of rocking.

And don't forget the swing, oh, please don't forget the porch swing. Days become swirls of lovely colors in the sway of a porch swing. The creaking becomes a sweet melody that allows one to ruminate rhythmically. And everyone knows a proper porch swing comes arrayed with pillows for those delicious moments when one successfully rocks oneself to sleep. The swing is the porch's poetry.

❤ *Lesson* ❤

Yes, a porch is a good thing. How about yours? Is it all set to offer an array of services to you and yours? It can be a place to receive guests and packages. A place to sip tea and visit. A grand place to take meals, park boots, sneak naps, read books, work puzzles, write letters, and watch for guests. But my favorite porch feature is that of a visible sign of refuge and shelter.

Scripture says the Lord God is a refuge and a shelter to those seeking safety. "How priceless is your unfailing love! Both high and low among men find refuge in the shadow of your wings" (Psalm 36:7). During inclement times we can go to Him, and He allows us to slip under his wings. Trust me, this is even better than a porch swing!

"What have we to expect? Anything. What have we to hope for? Everything. What have we to fear? Nothing."
—Edward B. Pusey

❤ Journal Exercise ❤

Is it easy or difficult for you to imagine yourself cuddled beside Jesus on a porch swing? What makes it easy? What makes it difficult? Can you imagine Him wrapping His arms of love around you? Is that easier during the happy times or the hard times? Write a description of how you and He would sit together in a porch swing, including your conversation as you sit sipping iced tea or a flavored coffee together. —KCM

Desires Of The Heart

Maureen Stirsman

Delight yourself in the LORD and he will give you the desires of your heart.
Psalm 37:4

My firstborn son, David, lived only half an hour. I never saw his face, never held his tiny body. Little was known about spina bifida in 1957.

My mother packed away our Christmas ornaments and the never-worn baby clothes, while my husband, Tom, and I tried to put the pieces of our lives together.

Two years went by. On September 22, 1959, I was in labor again—this time in Erie, Pennsylvania, where I was staying with my family while Tom served in the U.S. Army in Massachusetts.

When I heard baby Mark's cry I thought everything was fine. He was alive, yes, but also a victim of spina bifida. I was only twenty-two years old, and my heart broke again. My pastor, Ed Fuller, came to my hospital room and read Psalm 37:4, "Delight yourself in the LORD and he will give you the desires of your heart." The words reached my ears as though through earmuffs. But what Ed read was God's Word and truth. I believed in the Lord and knew our David was with Him. I feared that soon Mark would be in heaven, too.

I held him only twice during the three months of his life. Once again the baby clothes were packed away. A large hole in my heart bled. I thought I would never laugh again.

We were childless, but my heart's desire was for children! What was God going to do? Then the thought came—from Him—adoption!

One Wednesday evening thirteen months later our telephone rang. "We have a six-month-old baby girl for you," the caller said. I held my breath. "Can you come on Tuesday to see her?" *I'll be there if I have to walk on nails,* I thought.

Tom and I fell in love with Susan the minute we saw her face. She fit into my arms as though she were custom-made.

In 1964 God completed our family when we received Thomas. He was two and a half months old when we saw him for the first time. We loved him immediately.

Now our grandson, Matthew, has celebrated his twelfth birthday on the same weekend that Tom baptized him.

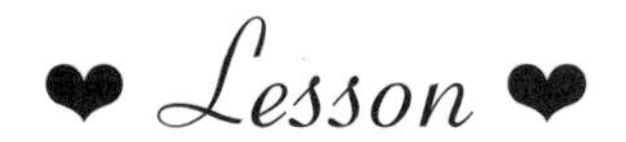

The promise in this Psalm can be your promise also. The loving Lord can help you to bear the pain of loss even if you feel healing is impossible. He will enable you to endure and to trust him more fully because of your experiences. He will bless you, and someday you will recognize that blessing. Maybe you will be a teacher, a youth leader, a wonderful aunt, or a good neighbor. This one thing I know—God is good and He is the author of delight.

"Lay them quietly at His feet
one by one:
each desire, however sweet,
just begun."
—Ruth Bell Graham

❤ Journal Exercise ❤

What desire of yours has not been realized? How has that made you feel about God and His plan for you? List the advantages of having an eternal perspective and the disadvantages of having an earthly perspective. When you think of your unmet desires, how can you choose an eternal perspective? —KCM

Faith Through Failure

Ida Rose Heckard

**Commit your way to the LORD; trust in him and he will do this:
He will make your righteousness shine like the dawn,
the justice of your cause like the noonday sun.
Psalm 37:5–6**

As a school psychologist for a large district, I had evaluated a severely handicapped child whose mother was battling our district. My evaluation supported her position. However, my supervisor didn't want to provide the services Andrew needed. When she pressured me to alter my findings, her fury with my unwillingness to lie permeated our relationship. I contended with false accusations. Defending myself was futile.

I spent hours crying out to God. "Should my faith cost me my job? How can I be a good witness when I feel like this?"

Each day the Lord took me to Psalm 37. Clinging to those promises strengthened me, but also confused me. "Lord," I prayed, "I don't want vindication. I just want Andrew to get an appropriate education. I'm committing my way to You but I don't see the promised results of shining righteousness."

During several tense meetings, with Andrew's mother present, my supervisor was openly hostile to me. Eventually Andrew received what he needed, but I continued to be harassed at the office for months. Finally, my husband and I decided I should resign. I felt like a failure.

On my last day, each note from a parent and each child's drawing added to my sense of failure. I tried to see things from God's perspective, but I wondered if the price of faith was worth it—especially for an issue with no eternal consequence.

The intercom interrupted my thoughts. "Mrs. Heckard?" called the school's secretary. "There's someone here to see you."

Curious, I headed for the office. Through the windows I saw Andrew's mother. "These are for you," she said, handing me a bouquet of flowers. In my office, we sat down amidst the boxes and she asked, "I don't understand, why did you do this for us?"

"Because of my faith in Jesus and because Andrew is precious in God's sight. I'm praying for both of you to know God's love."

Dabbing her tears, she said, "A friend has just invited us to church and now I know I have to go." As she turned to leave I thanked her for the flowers. "Oh, they're not from me," she said with a smile. "They're from Andy. If he could understand what you've done for him, he would have bought them for you."

❤ Lesson ❤

Before he became Israel's king, David, wrote Psalm 37. Amid seeming failure and unjust humiliation, David could have killed Saul to get the kingdom. But David committed his ways to the Lord.

When we trust ourselves to God's care no matter what, we may look like foolish failures. But the Lord becomes our righteousness, shining through us as the noonday sun. I left work that day with flowers, but my most prized possession was the knowledge that God's righteousness had flowed through me to touch a life. The One in whom I'd trusted hadn't failed at all.

"Faith means trusting in advance what will only
make sense in reverse."
—Philip Yancey

❤ Journal Exercise ❤

How do you define success? How do you think God defines success? Has there been a time when you thought you had failed and yet God revealed a different definition of success in that situation? Are you feeling like a failure right now? How does God want your righteousness to shine like the noonday sun in that situation? —KCM

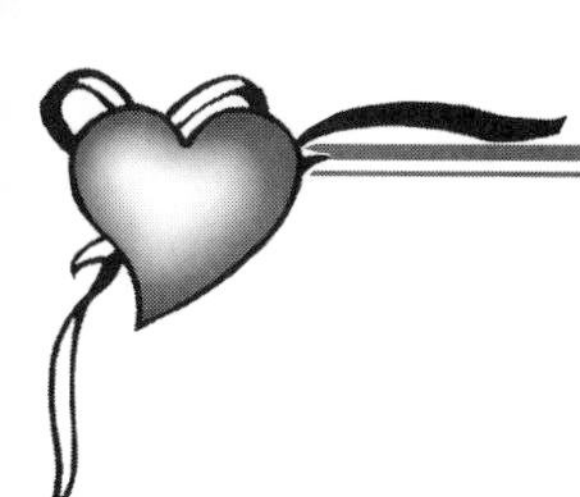

God's Delight

Sheila S. Hudson

If the LORD delights in a man's way, he makes his steps firm; though he stumble, he will not fall, for the LORD upholds him with his hand.
Psalm 37:23–24

Being a grandmother is the most wonderful position I have ever been privileged to hold. When I spend time with my oldest grandson, Jonathan, I feel as though I've been given a glimpse into God's heart. I delight in Jonathan. His slightest wish is my command and everything else goes "on hold" when he visits.

Jonathan Hudson Berry is two years old. Most of the time he is an affectionate, obedient, and cooperative toddler, but occasionally his rebellious side reasserts itself and the battle for independence is on. When he disobeys, I have to correct him, but I *still* love him. I'm just frustrated or disappointed in his behavior. I may warn him of hurts or punishment but when his stubbornness wins the battle, Jonathan gets into trouble.

When he's older, I'm sure we'll disagree. Jonathan will think I'm as old-fashioned as snail mail. But how he feels won't alter the fact that I love him and want the best for him. I'll always delight in him because he is a special person in my life. No matter how tired I am, if my head hurts, or a deadline looms, if Jonathan wants Mimi to read a story or bake cookies, I'm there.

Spending time with my grandchildren helps me know a little of how God must feel. The Psalmist describes God's love and

delight in us, His children, in the same way. God loves me no matter what. There are times I do and say things that are not attractive, but God still loves me. I fail, but His hand lifts me up. I look to Him for wisdom, for help, for security, for mercy.

God hasn't ever let me down and He offers me unconditional love. He doesn't mind if I am twenty pounds overweight or haven't reached last year's goals. God is the model parent. Because of His great love, I want very much to please Him. My actions have nothing to do with fear, and everything to do with love. I want God to delight in me just as I delight in my grandchildren.

He delights in you too, and wants you to experience His unconditional, "doting grandparent" love.

"Perfect love sometimes does not come
until the first grandchild."
—Welsh proverb

❤ Journal Exercise ❤

Did you experience as a child the unconditional love of a grandparent? How did he or she express that love? If you didn't, what would you have enjoyed about having such a loving grandparent? Like a good grandparent, God balances love and discipline. How do you see God doing that in your life? If you're a grandparent, how do you want to have the same balance toward your grandchildren? —KCM

The Great Dumpster Adventure

Sheila Rabe

The mouth of the righteous man utters wisdom, and his tongue speaks what is just. The law of his God is in his heart; his feet do not slip.
Psalm 37:30–31

It was time to go to the dump. Both the slaves (my children) were busy elsewhere, so I rode shotgun with my husband. Actually, I had never been to the dump before, and it sounded like fun, in a strange sort of way. We loaded the car trunk with recyclable goodies, and off we went.

The dump was a vast expanse of property. One area held two mammoth pits for garbage. Another, the recycling station, offered a series of slightly smaller pits with dumpsters fitted neatly into them like gigantic monsters with open mouths, waiting to be fed. Each monster preferred a different kind of food: green glass, pop cans, plastic milk cartons, or paper. Like the animals at the zoo, each had been cordoned off by a little fence of wire cable stretched between two posts. I hauled out a bag of milk cartons and wandered off to feed the milk carton monster.

Oops! A tuna can fell into the milk carton dumpster. I had heard from my children that the dump managers get angry with people who feed the wrong food to the monsters, so I stepped over the barrier, grabbed hold of the cable to secure myself, and daintily leaned in to retrieve my misplaced debris. *How far could that can have gone?* I leaned in farther.

Suddenly, I pitched downward. Frantic, I clutched the wire cable, but I kept going. The next thing I knew, slipping and sliding, I was hip deep in milk cartons.

I looked up to where I had been standing. There on the ground lay the wire cable, limp and useless—rather like me when my husband tried to haul me out. Hysterical laughter, I have learned, renders a person caught in a dumpster a total dead weight.

Once safely out of the pit, and smelling so lovely, I examined the fence which had looked so secure. The wooden post to which that sturdy cable was attached had not been anchored to the ground. My weight on the wire had been too much for it, and, under the pressure, it had fallen over, abandoning me to the monster.

❤ Lesson ❤

As we drove home, windows open, I realized how easy it is for us to fall into messes when we lean on our own shaky wisdom or build on a foundation other than God's Word. Conversely, we are blessed when we apply His principles to our lives.

The morals of our culture shift, making wise life choices a challenge. One wrong step can land us heart deep in unhappiness. Our own feelings, even others' advice, can prove as untrustworthy as the unanchored cable I had depended on to hold me.

Only one lifeline always holds secure; only one plan for living can keep us from falling into ugly messes. The Psalmist identified the Word of God as the anchor of the righteous person. Following our loving heavenly Father's instructions for living will prevent our spiritual walk from slipping on the world's shaky ground. Grasping His guidelines will keep us out of life's dumpsters.

What are you holding onto? An earthly cable that isn't secured, or God's eternal laws that never change and always give support?

"We get our moral bearings by looking at God."
—A. W. Tozer

❤ Journal Exercise ❤

What "laws" of the world do you see other people seeking as a source of security? Which ones have you grabbed at in the past? What happened? What changed when you held onto God's immutable principles? If you're being tempted right now to clutch onto an earthly cable, what Scripture can you find to help you reach out and grasp God's lifeline? —KCM

Answer To Praise!

Pamela F. Dowd

I waited patiently for the LORD; he turned to me and heard my cry. He lifted me out of the slimy pit, out of the mud and mire; he set my feet on a rock and gave me a firm place to stand.
Psalm 40:1–2

Jackie, the newly hired first grade teacher, walked into my office and shut the door. With teardrops staining her cheeks she said, "I can't do this! I quit!"

"No!" As the principal of the school, a thousand thoughts bombarded me. *It's Thursday and school starts Monday! How am I supposed to find someone over the weekend who can please twenty discriminating private school parents? I don't even have another applicant!*

In one hour I was due to host the annual Principal's Luncheon at my home for the rest of the staff—twenty-eight hungry, eager teachers. What would I tell them? As soon as word of Jackie's resignation got out, my phone line would be jammed with calls from first-graders' parents. I tired to remain rational.

"We can handle whatever it is," I said trying to boost her confidence and mine. I expected her to nod in agreement.

Instead, she turned and left my office.

As I drove home, I considered my fate. The way I saw it, I had only two options: a quick nervous breakdown or a leaning-on-God praise session. I chose the less feasible of the two: worship. *After all,* I reminded myself, *self-pity never improves my attitude or provides any answers. Besides, I don't have time to fall apart, I have company coming.*

While preparing food for my guests, I stood at my kitchen sink with tears coursing down my cheeks. I began to choke out a song. My voice trembled, but somehow singing bolstered my confidence. I sandwiched prayers between the familiar praise choruses, sending them like helium balloons into the "only-God-can" zone.

That night, I called a public school teacher and asked if she knew anyone looking for a teaching position. She directed me to a newly retired first grade teacher with an excellent reputation. When I called Mrs. Peden, she quickly agreed to come for an interview. I slept well that night.

I hired her the next day. In less than twenty-four hours, God had provided the perfect teacher. Ora Nell Peden was the answer to *praise*!

❤ Lesson ❤

I'm not sure I had ever before chosen praise first, but I sure have since. I used to automatically slide right into worry at the first hint of trouble. But this time, standing at the sink, I realized God had given me a choice. I could believe the Bible or resort to fretting. His Word makes clear that He remains with us, comforts us, guides us, and goes before us, behind us, and hems us in. The Psalmist described it as being lifted up from a muddy pit. My mud pit was worry.

The Psalmist described what I discovered when I offered God my praise. God put a new song in my mouth, and as He did, my fears and worries dissolved like the soap bubbles in the sink.

What are you going through today that could use a touch of praise? Try it, and watch your attitude change.

"Let God perform His own beautiful music
on the strings of your heart."
—Raymond P. Brunk

❤ Journal Exercise ❤

When we're in a pit of worry or anxiety, we feel overwhelmed. At times like that, what is your first reaction? If it's not what you would like it to be, how can you choose praise instead? When you were successful at turning your heart immediately to trusting God, what made you choose that reaction? How can you repeat that more often? —KCM

WEEK FIVE

A Retreat To Remember

Laurie D. Jenkins

**As the deer pants for streams of water,
so my soul pants for you, O God.
Psalm 42:1**

On a cool, damp fall morning, a thin blanket of fog covered the surface of the small lake as the women gathered on the shore. They stood side by side, facing the still water and the surrounding hillside. Hardly a word was spoken as the women prepared their hearts for worship. Then, without microphones or musical accompaniment, singing replaced silence as they offered their hearts and voices to God.

After several choruses, a new song began as a deer appeared nearby, walking slowly down the gentle slope to the lake. It came toward the group and paused before turning back to the water's edge. Then the deer stepped into the lake and swam across, its head barely visible through the fog lingering above the water. Amazed at what they had witnessed, several women sighed aloud as the song continued. Tears appeared in the eyes of some, smiles on the faces of others.

It wasn't the deer's appearance that made this such a memorable experience; it wasn't even the deer swimming across the lake that created such reactions. It was the words of the song the women were singing at that moment, "As the deer panteth for the water, so my soul longeth after Thee. . . ."

The timing of it all was a reminder that there are no coincidences with God.

❤ Lesson ❤

Psalm 42:1 describes an intense spiritual thirst, an incredible desire to know God intimately as our source of hope and strength, our source of life. It suggests a longing to feel His presence.

Whether we are away on a retreat or at home during an ordinary day, God is actively involved in our lives. He reveals Himself in many ways. And He wants us to notice when He does.

That will happen when our heart's desire is as the Psalmist's—to know God better, to "pant" after Him because we are thirsty for the spiritual drink He offers. He may reveal Himself in the form of a brilliant sunrise—a reminder of His power and the beauty of His creation. Or He could burst suddenly upon our awareness when an automobile collision is avoided at the last possible instant—an example of His protection. Or He may use an unforgettable set of circumstances to remind us of Himself.

Like seeing a deer on the shore of a lake, while singing a song.

"When we seek God, He finds us."
—Frank Lednicky

❤ Journal Exercise ❤

When you're thirsty or hungry, what is the only thing you can think of? When you're spiritually thirsty or hungry, who is the only One you can think of? When have you found that to be true for you? Has it been in times of need or fullness? Describe how your "panting" is expressed and journal how you think God regards your thirstiness for Him. —KCM

Don't Make It Worse

Robert H. Schuller

Why are you downcast, O my soul? Why so disturbed within me? Put your hope in God, for I will yet praise him, my Savior and my God.
Psalm 42:11

We have the power to make any problem better or worse. We do this when we react positively or negatively. The normal reaction would be to feel threatened by the problem. Threatened people become angry people. Fearful people reflect hatred. Hatred and anger only aggravate the problem. They are not positive reactions. They will not help solve the problem.

So you are overweight? Don't hate yourself for eating so much. That will not help you one bit.

Unemployed? Don't hate your company for laying you off. Likewise, don't hate your country for not coming through with a job offer, or your community for having an I-don't-care attitude about the unemployed.

Coach John Wooden chalked up a string of victories while he coached the famed University of California at Los Angeles basketball team. I once heard him say, "Nobody is defeated until he starts blaming somebody else."

My advice is, "Don't fix the blame; fix the problem." You begin fixing the problem when you begin to control your negative emotions.

If you've got a problem, don't add to it. Don't make your problem worse by aggravating it with self-pity, jealousy, cynicism, hatred, anger, or lack of positive faith in the future.

❤ Lesson ❤

Just like Dr. Schuller and the Psalmist tell us, we each have a choice how we're going to think. We do have an option! Praising God is the best possible way to stop focusing on the problem and instead get ready to fix the problem.

If we continue to focus on the problem, we're really saying God isn't powerful enough. But thinking of God's power and focusing on His other incredible attributes is what praise is all about. It'll bring us to the point of confidence in Him and diminish our hopelessness.

As soon as you recognize you're getting into the dumps, make a choice to praise God. You may find your disturbed soul feeling a lot better.—KCM

"Anger: an acid that can do more harm to the vessel in which it is stored than to anything on which it is poured."
—Unknown

❤ Journal Exercise ❤

Why do you think blaming others is so easy to do? What is your first response? What does blaming others say about the person doing the finger-pointing? Since God is sovereign—completely in control—what are we saying about Him when we fix blame? If you're blaming others about some situation right now, what are you going to do about it? —KCM

Anywhere But Germany

Corrie ten Boom

For this God is our God for ever and ever:
he will be our guide even to the end.
Psalm 48:14

When I left the concentration camp during the war, I said: "Now I will travel all over the world, and I shall go wherever God leads me. But I hope that He will never send me to Germany." Because of my experiences in prisons I had a distorted picture of Germany, which was not surprising.

So my obedience was limited: "Everywhere, Lord, but Germany." Then I went to America and when I asked for guidance, I did not receive an answer. That was very hard. Suddenly I asked: "Lord, is there perhaps a sin between You and me?" The answer was very clear: Germany. Then I understood and I said: "Lord, then also to Germany."

I went to Germany and found my enemies, but also many friends. In a sense I had more open doors in Germany than anywhere else in the world. And there I experienced that if you love your enemies you touch the ocean of God's love as never before.

So I learned my lesson: Obedience—not "Yes, but," but "Yes, Father."

God guides in a threefold way—first in our prayer time; second by His Word, the Bible; and third, by the circumstances. It is wonderful that in our prayers we not only speak but can also listen. We cannot do so at once; we must get accustomed to it.

❤ Lesson ❤

Each of us is often like Corrie ten Boom. We put parameters and restrictions on our obedience—and yet we still think we're being obedient. We just can't imagine that God wouldn't want the same thing for us as we want. Yet, He knows what is best, and at times, He says, "Yes, you'll go even to Germany." And when He does, He brings more blessings than we ever thought possible.

Being willing to do whatever God wants is the requirement for hearing God's guidance. The words of the Psalmist could refer to God being our guide even to the end of where we thought we could never go. And when we obey, we'll find that we know Him more as a great God than ever before. —KCM

"Wherever God has placed a period, don't try to change it to a question mark."
—Unknown

❤ Journal Exercise ❤

Who is your role model of obedience to the Lord? If you've never expressed your appreciation to him/her for that example, why not write a note? In what way would you like to emulate him/her? Is God nudging your heart to go to "Germany"? What will you do about it? —KCM

My Thankful Heart

Nanette Thorsen-Snipes

Sacrifice thank offerings to God, fulfill your vows to the Most High, and call upon me in the day of trouble; I will deliver you, and you will honor me.
Psalm 50:14–15

Thanksgiving—a day for giving thanks to the Lord. I fished another boiled egg from the pan and began shelling. Tossing the half-peeled egg into the pan, I wiped my tears on my sleeve.

I picked up the hospital bracelet my teenaged daughter, Jamie, had just taken off and threw it into the trash. Two days before, I had rushed her to the emergency room. For nine hours I waited while the doctors ruled out ulcers, kidney problems, stomach virus, and pelvic infection. About midday, my family doctor announced she had appendicitis.

I had hoped the proposed holiday activities at my son's house would keep me busy, so I wouldn't remember that Thanksgiving was the time of year my former husband, my boys' father, chose to commit suicide. Now, because of her surgery, Jamie would be unable to make the trip.

Bad memories of a former Thanksgiving lingered in my mind. My head pounded. Fresh tears slid down my face as I dialed my next-door neighbor. "Donna, do you have any aspirin?" I asked, trying to keep my voice from quivering.

"No, but I'll be glad to pick some up for you," she said cheerily.

"Thank you, but I'm going out anyway." My voice cracked as I added, "This is just not a good day for me." I hung up the phone. Nothing had gone right. Thanksgiving? I was incapable of being thankful for anything.

I drove alone to the store, my nose still red from crying. I felt so tired, so exhausted from the ordeal at the hospital. I wondered how I'd ever pull off a decent Thanksgiving at home. I wanted to call out to God, but I was full of self-pity. All I wanted to do was crawl into bed.

Pulling into the carport, I noticed a pot of gaily wrapped daisies by my back door. *Jamie is so well loved,* I thought. *Another friend has brought her flowers.* I brought the pot inside and set it on the table.

To my surprise, the piece of paper in the pot had my name on it. "Remember, His strength is perfect when our strength is gone," it read, "From Donna."

I touched the soft petals of a daisy thinking how self-centered I'd been and whispered a prayer of thanksgiving for a neighbor who cared enough to share the love of God with me.

❤ Lesson ❤

Sometimes, when we can't get beyond self-pity, God provides an act of kindness from an unexpected source to bring us back to Jesus—the real focus. When we slip away from Him, God admonishes us to "call upon him in the day of trouble."

"The longer we dwell on our misfortunes, the greater is their power to harm us."
—Voltaire

❤ Journal Exercise ❤

When do you find self-pity overwhelming you the most? What seems to feed your self-pity? What do you usually do in response? If it isn't calling upon God, why not? What do you think He wants you to do? Be specific. Journal about a time that God reached out to you during one of those self-pity times. —KCM

The Rewards Of Praising God

Anita J. Anderson

He who sacrifices thank offerings honors me, and he prepares the way so that I may show him the salvation of God.
Psalm 50:23

I was awakened in the gray light of dawn by piercing, sharp pains in my left wrist. Tears came to my eyes as I dreaded going through another day doing household tasks with such severe discomfort. Medicine barely relieved the agony from the irritated nerves in my wrist. I had pressing spring garden work to do, but the pain was wearing me down emotionally as well as physically.

I lay in bed praying quietly to the Lord for help as my husband slept beside me. I didn't even want to maneuver myself out of bed with that painful wrist. Then, I heard the inaudible voice of the Lord say, "Praise Me."

Although I did not understand why the Lord was telling me to do this, I started praising Him. It was easy to think of things that I appreciated about Him—His sovereignty, graciousness, patience, kindness, and so many other wonderful attributes. In addition, I could thank Him for so many good things in my life. As I did so, I began to feel a warm balm flood over my arms and down into my wrists and hands. Soon, the pain in my left wrist disappeared. I felt bathed in warmth, soothed and relieved.

I wiggled my wrist. It didn't hurt anymore! Joy surged up in me so strongly that I jumped out of bed and hurried downstairs so that I could praise the Lord more exuberantly. In the weeks that followed the pain in my wrist never returned. More than two years later, it remains healed.

❤ Lesson ❤

In Psalm 50:23, God says that when we sacrifice by giving thank offerings (or as it is stated in the NKJV "whoever offers praise"), the Lord will show us His salvation. Why is praising Him sometimes a sacrifice? When I was in pain, it was not a natural time to give praise or thanks to the Lord; my thoughts were too focused on my pain. In order to praise the Lord I had to sacrifice my focus on my physical needs and focus on Him.

According to the Psalmist's words, offering thanks prepares the way for God to show salvation to us. I was taught as a child that the word "salvation" meant that my soul was prevented from going to hell when I died. However, the Hebrew definition contains much more. The Hebrew word for salvation in Psalm 50:23 is yesha, which means liberty—deliverance as well as the more familiar words "safety" and "salvation." God comes into our lives when we ask Him to and saves us from eternal separation from Himself. He can also choose to begin the process of freeing our body, soul, and spirit from sin's bondage in this present life.

God healed my left wrist out of His mercy and loving-kindness when I was willing to please Him with praise instead of focusing on myself. But of even greater value was my learning how close God actually is to me—living in the now, in relationship with me. The experience drew me closer to Him.

The next time you're focusing on yourself, praise and thank God instead.

"Healing and health are of little value if they do not glorify God and serve to unite us more closely with Him."
—Andrew Murray

❤ Journal Exercise ❤

What does it mean to you to "praise" God? How are praise and giving thanks different? Write here a list of the qualities of God you most appreciate. Then write a list of the things you appreciate and thank God for in your life. Is it much of a "sacrifice" to do that? If so, how will you make the choice anyway?
—KCM

Speaking the Truth

Doris Schuchard

**Surely you desire truth in the inner parts; you teach me wisdom in the inmost place.
Psalm 51:6**

The first day of my son's eighth grade year should have been one of happiness and expectation. Instead, I was to hear on a daily basis, "I hate you. Only mean parents would do this to me!"

"This" was a planned move to Atlanta from our home in the Midwest. My husband had already started his new job while the children and I stayed behind to sell the house. It wasn't an easy decision. We had toyed with the idea of not putting the house on the market till the children completed the school year, but being separated that long seemed an even greater hardship.

So here I was, ferrying the kids to school and sports, showing the house, researching the neighborhoods and schools of our new home, and trying to deal with a depressed and angry son. I worried when Matthew talked of running away or hurting himself. He couldn't see the future. For all he knew, his life would end the day we moved.

After walking on eggshells with him, I was unprepared for what happened a few months later when we finally moved. Matthew had spent every day holed up inside, watching TV, playing video games, and surfing the internet. Finally, one warm winter day we pushed him out the door. "Ride your bike, go rollerblading, or just take a walk and explore your new neighborhood."

An hour later he returned. "I was just playing football with the guys down the street," he mentioned casually as he grabbed a snack. "And they invited me to walk to school with them."

That was the turning point. It didn't take Matthew long to fit in—he even began to smile again. And I knew he had adjusted to his home when his confirmation class was asked to give their testimonies in church. I rejoiced with him when he stood up and shared, "There is always a reason for something happening to me. I was very worried about life here. Moving was a traumatic experience. But God has led me through and now I like it here. God has a plan for me—He always works for the good of those who love Him."

Where did all this sudden wisdom come from? Maybe allowing him to vent his frustrations to me helped him. I lent a listening ear to all his fears, just as God listens when we whine. Maybe it's simpler than that. God is a God of miracles and new beginnings. Sometimes we need to take a step back and let God work. Then, like the Psalmist, our hearts will rejoice in recognizing that wisdom comes from knowing God.

"A child should always say what's true."
—Robert Louis Stevenson

❤ Journal Exercise ❤

If there is a person who seems to lack the wisdom you desire for them, how have you responded to them? How does God want you to respond to them, if He is the source of true wisdom? Write your reflection here of asking for God's wisdom in knowing how to react and in calling upon God's power to do so. —KCM

WEEK SIX

Vacation Classroom

Ted Weaver

You do not delight in sacrifice, or I would bring it; you do not take pleasure in burnt offerings. The sacrifices of God are a broken spirit; a broken and contrite heart, O God, you will not despise.
Psalm 51:16–17

Jimmy was sick and getting worse with a high fever. This could ruin our rare family vacation in New Mexico's beautiful cool pines. We were several hundred miles from home, knew no one, and were in an isolated mountain cabin. As new Christians we prayed, but Jimmy continued to get worse so, in desperation, I went into another room to pray.

God directed me to reflect on the activities of the day, which had begun in a national forest. We had dug up several trees for our Texas yard in defiance of large signs prohibiting it. We had gone on to White Sands National Monument where we again violated clear regulations, taking several large buckets of the unique white sand.

Later in the day, I had been involved in a heated disagreement with a grocery store clerk. I had been harsh, loud, and rude with the lady over a dispute concerning the price of sodas.

Our two children had participated in or witnessed all these incidents. As I prayed about Jimmy's illness, God convicted me of my sins. I repented and promised the Lord that I'd make restitution. God was gracious. I believe He rewarded me by breaking Jimmy's fever and causing him to sleep peacefully.

Early the next morning, we returned to the national forest where we replanted the trees in the same holes from which we had taken them. We then took the stolen sand to the Park Ranger's station and with the family watching, I acknowledged having taken it. The Ranger was surprised, stating that most everyone took sand and for us to come all the way back to return it was unique.

We proceeded to the grocery store. The clerk's remembrance of the previous day was obvious when she saw me; she was all business with no smiles. As she completed the last customer before us, we moved directly in front of her. I apologized for my rudeness and asked her forgiveness. She was stunned and could only nod that she would accept the apology and forgive me. As we walked away from the checkout area, I glanced back over my shoulder and saw that she was looking at us. She waved good-bye.

Our vacation was cut short by going to the same places twice, but the lessons learned were worth it.

I could have easily repented in my heart, but a private confession wouldn't have shown the broken spirit and contrite heart that the Psalmist speaks of as so important to God. My family benefited from my example of making public confessions.

God delights in and never refuses the offering of a broken spirit and contrite heart. We can think that sacrificing something will please God, but it must be accompanied by a repentant heart.

The truly amazing thing is that he takes the pieces of our broken hearts and lovingly pours His forgiveness over them—restoring us to wholeness and joy.

"What we fail to repent of we are destined to repeat."
—Unknown

❤ Journal Exercise ❤

Make a list of the ways people avoid taking responsibility for their sins. Put a check mark by those that you have used. Make another list of the reasons we don't want to confess our sins. What are the benefits of confession? Do you think they are worth the confession? If there is something that you need to confess, write your feelings to God and then memorize a Scripture that refers to God's forgiveness. —KCM

Growling Stomachs And Groaning Souls

Ginny Yttrup

O God, you are my God, earnestly I seek you; my soul thirsts for you, my body longs for you, in a dry and weary land where there is no water, . . . My soul will be satisfied as with the richest of foods; with singing lips my mouth will praise you.
Psalm 63:1, 5

Last year, driving from southern California to northern California, I became hungry and thirsty. In the midst of a desolate valley, I longed for French fries and a soda. Just one fry would have sufficed! I lustfully recalled the smell of fresh potatoes sizzling in hot grease. The sound of bubbling soda pouring over crackling ice tantalized my mind. The sight of golden arches arising from the endless valley farmlands became my desert mirage. How I longed to be filled.

It was hours, or seemingly so—one's perception of time is altered in such circumstances—before my eyes rested on the blessed sign indicating that food was just ahead. Finally, my longings would be satisfied!

Much to my dismay, the fast-food establishment served up a limp and saltless fry! And my soda, while satisfying for the moment, left me thirsting for water. Disgruntled, I continued my trek homeward, unsatisfied.

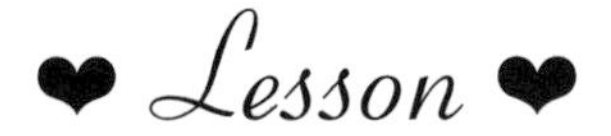

Lesson

Often, it seems, I find myself dismayed, discouraged, and unsatisfied. Occasionally, a crisp and salty French fry will satisfy my longings. More often than not, however, my longings are those of a groaning soul, rather than of a growling stomach. I hunger and thirst for understanding, acceptance, and love, and I frantically search for a quick fix to ease my painful emotions.

King David, who wrote Psalm 63, understood the soul's hunger for love. Perhaps David, like me, sometimes sought a quick fix for his anguished heart. I wonder if his midnight encounter with Bathsheba was an attempt to fix or numb his lonely soul. Unfortunately, David's sin with glaring consequences proved a feeble fix. My fixes are feeble, too!

Although David, like each of us, had times of weakness, ultimately he knew the quenching attributes of God and sought Him earnestly. In a "dry and weary land," David thirsted for God; his body longed for God. And he was satisfied. Psalm 63:5 records David's satisfaction.

As I contemplate my dislike of mild discomfort, especially a growling stomach, I realize that discomfort prompts me to seek relief. When I, like David, earnestly seek God to fill me, my soul will be satisfied beyond my greatest desire.

How's your spiritual thirst? Are you trying to cover it with temporary earthly delights? Not even French fries will relieve it. Seek God instead.

Perhaps being hungry and thirsty aren't as bad as I thought.

"Oh God, the Triune God, I want to want Thee; I long to be filled with longing; I thirst to be made more thirsty still.
Show me Thy glory, I pray . . ."
—A. W. Tozer

❤ Journal Exercise ❤

How does your spiritual appetite express itself? With what earthly delights do you try to satisfy your spiritual longings? Do they work? Of the spiritual disciplines (prayer, Bible study, meditation, Scripture memorization, fasting, etc.), which do you practice? How does it satisfy? Which one would you like to develop more in your life? —KCM

Night Watches

Elsie H. Brunk

On my bed I remember you; I think of you through the watches of the night.
Psalm 63:6

I awoke in the night and couldn't seem to get comfortable again. I was recovering from surgery that I had had two weeks earlier. Because I had suspected that all was not well with my recovery, I had made an appointment with a different surgeon.

The surgery itself was considered minor, but because of the way it had been done, my pain had been major! Fears began to flood my mind. *Will the examination tomorrow be painful too? What will the doctor find? Am I healing? Will there be need for further surgery?*

My thoughts turned to God, my true source of help in time of trouble. *Oh God, You know that I can't stand the thought of any more pain right now. But You know what is best for me. Please take my fears and worries and give me Your peace.* Then I chose to praise Him. My body relaxed, and I went back to sleep.

At my appointment the next day, the doctor simply looked at the area of surgery and said, "I can see you're still hurting. I'll give you two more weeks to heal and then we'll check you further."

How thankful I was for that reprieve!

There have been many nights in my life when I've had plenty to worry about. I've found that if I want to have a peaceful sleep at those times, I must focus my mind on God, give Him my

fears and anxieties, and then spend my "night watches" praising Him. Sometimes I simply repeat the name of "Jesus" over and over as I focus my mind on Him. Each time I've "remembered God on my bed" and thought of Him in the "night watches"—as the Psalmist did—and chosen to trust Him rather than entertain worries and fears, I've been able to sleep peacefully.

God wants us to think of Him in those dark hours of the night when our thoughts threaten to overwhelm us. God wants us to trust Him.

The next time fears, worries, and negative thoughts try to rob you of sleep, choose to focus your thoughts on God and spend time thanking and praising Him. You may be surprised at how quickly you fall asleep.

"If we worry, we don't trust. If we trust, we don't worry."
—Unknown

❤ Journal Exercise ❤

There's something about the nighttime that makes all our fears and anxieties surface with greater power. Does that happen to you? What seems to give the worries more strength? Is it easy or difficult to focus on the Lord at those times? How could 2 Corinthians 10:5 make you even stronger than those fears? What will you do the next time you awaken with fear? —KCM

Hand In Hand

Brenda Jank

Because you are my help, I sing in the shadow of your wings. My soul clings to you; your right hand upholds me.
Psalm 63:7–8

My four-year-old son, Samuel, and I were enjoying a morning at a local children's museum. A new exhibit had opened, and Sam could barely contain his excitement at the prospect of exploring the inside of this beautiful miniature home. Once inside we were greeted, not by the quaintness of little rooms and little furniture as we had expected, but by a little doorway leading to a dark tunnel. I had no idea what we might encounter, but Sam seemed up to the challenge. So, side by side and hand in hand (not an easy feat while crawling on all fours) we entered the blackness.

Samuel instantly drew back. "Mommy, I don't like this!"

"It's very dark inside, isn't it, Sam? But it's a tunnel, and it will lead us through the house and out the door on the other side. It's going to be very dark and we won't be able to see, but if you want to go, I'll be right here and I'll hold your hand the whole time."

He sat and thought for a minute. He decided to try. Inch by inch we crept inside. Suddenly, Samuel let out an anguished sob, followed by a steady stream of loud, wailing cries. The darkness had overwhelmed him.

"Sam, Samuel, listen to me . . . . This is your mommy! You can't see me but I am right here! Do you feel my hand? This is my hand! I am right here."

Instantly, he became calm. In an unbelievably chipper voice he replied, "Oh, Mommy! I just forgot I was holding your hand."

With confidence and courage my little adventurer crawled on, and we reached our goal. Once outside the tunnel in the bright, wonderful light, we celebrated the accomplishment!

❤ Lesson ❤

Life is an adventure, yet some "seasons" are overwhelming. The months seem endless and the heartache unrelenting. We travel onward. Our cries of anguish come in many forms . . . worries through sleepless nights . . . angry, hurtful words that spill out of our mouths . . . unhealthy appetites for attention, cookies, or credit cards.

There are no easy answers at times like this. Working our way through the dark tunnels of our lives is a slow, step-by-step process of staying close to the One who longs to hold our hand. His touch is gentle and reassuring. He won't let go! We must remember that nails didn't hold Him to the cross two thousand years ago—it was His love.

Today, that love still echoes through the corridors of our lives, no matter how dark and unfamiliar. The Psalmist writes of God's right hand upholding us. Jesus says to us, "Dear one, listen to me . . . this is Jesus! You can't see me but I am right here! Do you feel my hand . . . the one with the scar? This is my hand. I am beside you!"

"Lord, I crawled across the barrenness to You with my empty cup uncertain in asking any small drop of refreshment. If only I had known You better I'd have come running with a bucket."
—Nancy Spiegelberg and Dorothy Purdy

❤ Journal Exercise ❤

Do you feel God's hand in yours right now? Make a list of the ways God has led you even when you didn't think He was with you. Is there an area of your life where it seems there's only darkness and His hand isn't holding yours? In what one small way can you know He's leading you through that dark tunnel? Write out your thanks to Him. —KCM

Water, Water Everywhere

Penny Schlaf Musco

Save me, O God, for the waters have come up to my neck. I sink in the miry depths, where there is no foothold. I have come into the deep waters; and floods engulf me.
Psalm 69:1–2

You might think that because I grew up on the west coast of Florida, I'd have learned how to swim early in life. But I was profoundly afraid of the water. That fear began when I was at a friend's house, standing next to the deep end of her pool, and she unaccountably pushed me in. I plunged beneath the surface and immediately panicked. I grabbed onto a nearby adult, who towed me to the shallow end. I stood there for a long time, trembling with fright.

By my senior year in college, I wanted to conquer that fear. With much trepidation, I signed up for a semester of swimming lessons. Not wanting the extra pressure of trying to make a decent grade, I used my one remaining pass/fail option (or was that sink or swim?)

Amazingly, I had fun! I mastered the basic strokes, then recklessly decided to keep going and enroll for another term, this time for a grade!

I should have quit while I was ahead. While perfecting our technique, the class also practiced diving, which I hated. Then we had to "drown-proof" ourselves by learning how to endure long periods of time in the water. In the old days, this was known as the "dead man's float," but was now called the "survival float."

To me, the exercise was pure torture. Moving through the water was one thing, but to relax with my face in the water, coming up every fifteen seconds for air, brought up all my old fears. Somehow I managed to get a B. I was awfully glad to be back on solid ground.

❤ *Lesson* ❤

Years later, when I read Psalm 69:1–2 for the first time, I was in the midst of a long siege of panic attacks and depression. This time it wasn't my body that fought drowning—it was my soul. A flood of anxious thoughts engulfed me day after day, and I groped for some secure foothold amidst the churning waters of my spirit.

Then I remembered my life vest—Scripture. I echoed David's despair in these verses.

God answered me and reminded me of His promise in Isaiah 43:2, "When you pass through the waters, I will be with you; and when you pass through the rivers, they will not sweep over you." I clung to that "flotation device," and eventually, despite repeated frenzied flailing, I bobbed back to the shore of peace and security once again.

There will always be floods in my life and yours, when we lose our grip on life, the very ground under our feet falls away, and an ocean washes over us. Treading water isn't fun, but we don't have to do it alone. The buoyancy of God's love and comfort will rescue us from the undertow of fear and lead us out of life's deep end.

"In the turmoil of life without, and bleak despair within,
it is always possible to turn aside and wait on God.
He will always turn up."
—Malcolm Muggeridge

❤ Journal Exercise ❤

Describe a time when you felt as though you were spiritually or emotionally drowning. What life vests did God provide for you? What promise did He give you to buoy you above the waves of hopelessness? How does the Lord want you to use that experience now to toss a life vest to someone else? Write a letter to a hurting person today and express your hope in God. —KCM

The Power Of Forgiveness

Max Lucado

Help us, O God our Savior, for the glory of your name; deliver us and forgive our sins for your name's sake.
Psalm 79:9

Recently I shared a meal with some friends. A husband and wife wanted to tell me about a storm they were weathering. Through a series of events, she learned of an act of infidelity that had occurred over a decade ago. He had made the mistake of thinking it'd be better not to tell her, so he didn't. But she found out. And as you can imagine, she was deeply hurt.

Through the advice of a counselor, the couple dropped everything and went away for several days. A decision had to be made. Would they flee, fight, or forgive? So they prayed. They talked. They walked. They reflected. In this case the wife was clearly in the right. She could have left. Women have done so for lesser reasons. Or she could have stayed and made his life a living hell. Other women have done that. But she chose a different response.

On the tenth night of their trip, my friend found a card on his pillow. On the card was a printed verse: "I'd rather do nothing with you than something without you." Beneath the verse she had written these words: *I forgive you. I love you. Let's move on.*

The card might as well have been a basin. And the pen might as well have been a pitcher of water, for out of it poured pure mercy, and with it she washed her husband's feet.

Certain conflicts can be resolved only with a basin of water. Are any relationships in your world thirsty for mercy? Are there any sitting around your table who need to be assured of your grace?

❤ Lesson ❤

As David wrote (and shouldn't he know, of all people?), God forgives us for His own sake. He wants to have fellowship with us because He loves us so much. Therefore, He longs to restore the relationship with us. Regardless of the depth of our sin, He offers His hand of forgiveness, as Max Lucado points out.

If we will do the same and move on, we'll find a peace that never would be available by withholding forgiveness. —KCM

"Relationships don't thrive because the guilty are punished but because the innocent are merciful."
—Max Lucado

❤ Journal Exercise ❤

Who in your world needs his or her pitcher filled with life-giving forgiveness? If you were to forgive, how would you communicate it? How do you think he/she would respond? How would you feel after you have forgiven? When have you experienced the pitcher of grace poured upon you from someone else? How did you feel? Define grace in your own words. —KCM

WEEK SEVEN

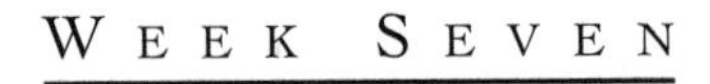

Trusting His Wisdom

Cindi McMenamin

No good thing does he withhold from those whose walk is blameless.
Psalm 84:11b

In the margin of my Bible, Psalm 84:11 is highlighted. I had claimed this promise as I prayed over and over to the Lord for Hugh to become my husband. Hugh was the man of God who had stolen my heart.

"Truly Hugh is a 'good thing' for me and surely I am walking uprightly," I prayed. "Certainly You will not withhold him from me." And God didn't. One year after I first prayed that promise, Hugh and I were married. And I have seen over the past twelve years how Hugh has been a "good thing" in my life.

When it came time to plan our second child, I remembered this promise and began to pray it over and over again. "Surely another child is a 'good thing,'" I prayed. "Surely I am walking uprightly. Certainly You will not withhold this 'good thing,' Lord." And yet God did. Year after year, and to this day, He has withheld from us a second child.

❤ Lesson ❤

I had to trust in the truth of this Psalm from God's perspective, not my own. If I am walking blameless before Him and something is truly good for me, He will not withhold it; that is His promise. But if He is withholding something from me, then I must conclude that it is not good for me, not at this time, and not in His perfect plan.

Today I see that God was preparing me for other things during those days when I had prayed for a second child. He saw that I would need to concentrate all my mothering efforts on my only daughter to keep her on the straight and narrow path. He determined it was "good" for me to give "birth" in other areas—a speaking ministry to women, a book about intimacy with God, and an understanding of the pain women feel during infertility. The "good thing" God blessed me with was not another child, but a more effective usefulness for Him.

Is God withholding something from you, even though you are walking blameless before Him? Perhaps He is waiting to deliver that blessing at the proper time. Or it could be that His wise, all-seeing eyes notice something that you don't. Trust His wisdom in withholding. It may lead to other blessings you haven't imagined!

"Good when He gives, supremely good,
Nor less when He denies.
Even crosses from His sovereign hand
Are blessings in disguise."
—Old hymn

❤ Journal Exercise ❤

How do you define "good" in your view of God? When has He withheld something from you that you thought was "good"? How did a better plan result? Is there something that you're asking for now that God is delaying in supplying? How does that make you feel? What do you think it means to walk "blameless"? Are you fulfilling your part of the promise? —KCM

"Coincidence"

Steven S. Bovia

If you make the Most High your dwelling—even the LORD who is my refuge—then no harm will befall you, no disaster will come near your tent.
Psalm 91:9–10

My son, Patrick, didn't like the "really ugly holly bush" (as he described it) at the side of his house. The previous owners had never trimmed it properly, so it grew in an unattractive, clumsy fashion. It was too close to the house and the roots would eventually ruin the foundation—solid reasons to eliminate the spindly mass. With much tenacity Patrick cut it back, then dug at it. He even attempted to pull out the roots. The holly continued to live, albeit smaller and less obtrusive than before.

One balmy summer afternoon, I got a call from Patrick announcing, "Carson fell out of the second story bedroom window."

"Oh no! How badly is he hurt?" I asked, as visions of my grandson flashed across my thoughts. He was a fearless, eighteen-month-old, blonde-haired boy with bright blue eyes and the heart of a champion. I imagined his small body with the kind of injuries I'd seen while serving in the military.

"He's got a couple of scratches on his face and arms," my son responded coolly. "Carson was playing in his bedroom while I was downstairs with the girls. We heard a whimpering outside the house. My mind said, *Carson,* and I made the half-second dash from the kitchen to the outside knowing what had happened. My fears were confirmed. Carson was standing in the yard with the window screen lying next to him."

"And he really wasn't hurt?" I asked, not understanding.

"Nothing serious. He apparently rode the screen down and landed on the holly bush, which rolled him off onto the ground."

"That's miraculous! What a blessing!" Then the irony struck me. "You mean that scraggly old holly bush saved his life?"

"Just one of God's 'coincidences,' isn't it, Dad?" he said with a catch in his voice.

"Yeah. . . . You told God 'thank you,' yet?" was all I could say.

"About a thousand times. And, there's been a change in plans."

"Plans?" I asked.

"Yea, Dad. Carson's room is going downstairs and that holly bush is staying."

❤ *Lesson* ❤

As the Psalmist points out, we only need to attempt to dwell with Him, in His house, under His guidance and He will protect us. That means we make our lives His dwelling and follow His instructions. Then he will spread out His grace upon all areas of our lives and be in charge of the "coincidences" so that we might identify His hand of protection upon us. We may still experience hard, hurtful things, but God will be in the midst of them.

What Patrick tried to eliminate, God used for good. Are you trying to eliminate something that God is saying, "leave alone?" You don't know how He may want to use that thing in your "dwelling." Trust that He's protecting you all along.

"I have held many things in my hands, and I have lost them all; but whatever I have placed in God's hands, that I still possess."
—Martin Luther

❤ Journal Exercise ❤

Who or what are you trying to control? Is it any "coincidence" that God is using the very thing that you are trying to control, maybe even eliminate? Can you see God's protection in the midst of something that seems to need to change? What is God really saying your attitude and actions should be? —KCM

Night Light

C. Ellen Watts

You will not fear the terror of night, nor the arrow that flies by day, nor the pestilence that stalks in the darkness, nor the plague that destroys at midday.
Psalm 91:5–6

My husband had been traveling for years for his company when the wife of one of his colleagues came to see me. Bitterness lined what could have been an attractive face as Lucinda complained that her Harry was away from home four nights a week. "Evenings are worst for me," she said. "Ellen, how are you able to cope?"

I replied calmly, "I guess I'm too busy to fret." But as soon as I spoke, I could tell my words struck her as uncaring. "But Lucinda, I do remember struggling. There were times, especially after the children were grown and gone, that I didn't want to be alone. But there is one thing that helped me cope."

Lucinda leaned forward to hear the secret.

"I asked God to protect me and to help me fill the hours with worthwhile activity."

❤ Lesson ❤

If your mate travels or works nights, or if you live alone, God doesn't want you to fear the night's darkness. He wants you to be content regardless of your circumstances. Here are some tips.

Accept your circumstances. *My husband is a corrosion specialist. Travel is as necessary to his work as is a quiet office* *to mine. Most of the time, your situation can't be changed. Accept your circumstances, knowing God can change them if He desires.*

Develop the relationship with your spouse. *My husband and I research the area where he'll travel. Such knowledge shortens the distance between us and provides for interesting conversation. Also, learn about your spouse's occupation.*

Never stop learning. *Enroll in a class. Choose a subject that interests you and get involved. Be honest about your hidden dreams and find a way to fulfill them.*

Adopt a craft or hobby. *I have crafted and stitched countless items, then donated them to boutiques that benefit others. One gentleman I know repairs toys for charity; a neighbor paints pottery.*

Invite guests to your home. *Entertain the "widows and orphans" for whom the Bible suggests we are responsible. Keep in mind that the lonely and alone are probably longing for fellowship and not fancy fixings—so keep it simple.*

Plan to grow spiritually. *Keeping in tune with God provides a solid base for contentment. Quiet evenings make both personal and group Bible study possible. In times of loneliness or fear, use your alone times to pray and read Scripture. Allow these circumstances to draw your heart closer to your heavenly Father.*

David, wrote about God's promise of protection and peace in his times of aloneness. We can claim the same promise.

"The secret of being miserable is to have leisure to bother about whether you are happy or not. The cure for it is occupation."
—George Bernard Shaw

❤ Journal Exercise ❤

When have you felt fearful? Are there any experiences from your childhood that contribute to your fear? What wrong assumption about God might be fueling your fear? Maybe you think He's not powerful enough to protect you. Maybe you think He won't care if you get hurt. Uncover the source of your fear and hand it to the Lord. —KCM

A Wing And A Prayer

Gail Black Kopf

For he will command his angels concerning you to guard you in all your ways.
Psalm 91:11

When I arrived home from church on a blustery night in January 1999, I felt God nudging me to call my older brother in Tennessee. I dialed, but after eight rings I was ready to hang up. Had I mistaken my own thoughts for God's?

Finally my brother's deep "Hello," answered, and I said, "Gene, it's Gail."

"I'm in the house by myself," he said. "I sent Anita and the kids to safety. They've spotted three tornadoes in our area. One's a half mile away. Can you hear the hail?"

My voice quavered. "Why didn't you leave with the others?"

"What if looters come through? Besides," he boasted with daredevil conviction, "if Elijah didn't mind going to heaven in a whirlwind, why should I?"

At the image of my burly, fifty-something brother being swept up in a whirlwind, we both broke into laughter. Gene asked, "Do you remember that day in Kansas?"

We briefly reminisced about that day forty years earlier when a black funnel had appeared in the winding country lane where we lived. We'd scrambled into the root cellar while it passed, then crawled out of our shelter to peer at the ravaged landscape. Miracle of miracles, our white farmhouse was still standing, but the three other houses on our road had disappeared.

"Well," I confessed, returning to the present, "something just told me to call you. Maybe so I could pray—"

A loud click severed our connection. *What can I do? I'm five hundred miles away in West Virginia.* "Pray," the quiet voice from within prompted.

"Please Lord, send angels to encircle Gene's home." I envisioned glistening angels with their huge wings outstretched, forming a windbreak around my brother's home.

Two agonizing hours dragged by before I could reach Gene again. He described the devastation: uprooted trees; downed electrical lines; broken windows; porches flattened by the tornado's swath; and awnings and swing sets, like colorful jackstraws, splayed across once tidy lawns in his neighborhood.

"What about your house?" I asked.

"That's the strange part," he said with a sense of wonder. "It's as if the wind veered right around us. Not even a flowerpot on the porch is overturned. Can you imagine that?"

❤ Lesson ❤

Angels, our ever-present guardians, are a very real force in God's kingdom. These invisible companions can move at the speed of light to guide and guard, comfort and console us. The Psalmist knew their power and confirms that God commands them to do His bidding. One of their primary responsibilities is to protect God's children.

Although we should not pray directly to angels, we can ask God to send them to protect us. When you find yourself in a dangerous situation, remember the truth of the Psalmist's words.

"[Angels] regard our safety, undertake our defense, direct our ways and exercise a constant solicitude that no evil befall us . . ."
—John Calvin

❤ Journal Exercise ❤

How do you feel about the idea of angels? Can you describe a time when you called upon God to send His angels to help or protect you? What happened? If you are skeptical about the existence of angels, on what do you base your opinion? What about the angels mentioned in the Bible? —KCM

Hidden Beauty of the Heart

Joan Clayton

They will still bear fruit in old age; they will stay fresh and green.
Psalm 92:14

"Aren't you the Mrs. Clayton that taught first grade some years ago?" a woman asked me in the grocery store not long ago.

"Yes," I replied trying to put a name with her face.

"Well, I hardly knew you," she said. "You don't look like you used to." She turned and walked away.

Now, I had two choices. I could hold onto the good day I'd been having so far, or I could become offended and wonder, *What in the world did she mean by* that *remark?"*

I chose to keep my good day. Actually, the woman did me a favor. She caused me to take my "spiritual temperature."

❤ Lesson ❤

Our culture puts a premium on youth and beauty. Television commercials are flooded with products that supposedly keep us young looking. Cosmetic surgery—enhancements, face lifts, nose jobs—is "in."

Yes, we should try to look our best, but to be preoccupied with youth and beauty to the point of near financial bankruptcy is disastrous. Deprivation diets to achieve the world's definition of beauty are totally unrealistic. The underlying message is, "You are not okay the way you are. You are not acceptable."

If we accept the world's definition of beauty, our self-esteem will diminish as we age. Not only could we feel we look "tacky," we might feel useless and unwanted. We may begin to think we aren't able to help others as we once did or "bear fruit" in old age.

But we are still important and useful to God. The Lord's plan for His children does not end with advancing age. People like Albert Einstein, Ben Franklin and Colonel Sanders made tremendous contributions to society in their golden years.

I love Caleb's attitude about older age. In Joshua 14:10–11, he declares that at 85, he is still just as strong and useful as ever. Yeah, Caleb! You're my kind of guy!

Some of the most beautiful people I know are older saints who have that radiant glow of Jesus. They are like palm trees. The older their dates, the sweeter they are. Their experiences are a wealth of knowledge and their walk with God gives great spiritual insights.

So the next time I see that lady in the store, I'm going to say, "Hi! Remember me? I'm the Mrs. Clayton who taught first grade many years ago. I know you didn't recognize me; a lot of time has gone by. But you should see me on the inside! My spirit is becoming younger and more beautiful by the minute. I am being changed from one degree of glory to another. Because of Jesus, I have the hidden beauty of the heart!"

"There will come a time when you believe everything is finished. That will be the beginning."
—Louis L'Amour

❤ Journal Exercise ❤

How do you feel about getting older? What do you think will be the advantages of older age? Disadvantages? What kind of "older" person do you want to be? Are there any patterns in your life now that could impede your attainment of the beautiful qualities you desire? What "fruit" would you like to bear in your advanced years? How are you nourishing the ground now for producing that fruit later? —KCM

I'm Falling, Lord

Kathy Collard Miller

**When I said, "My foot is slipping," your love,
O LORD, supported me.
Psalm 94:18**

My mother, my one-year-old daughter, Darcy, and I were visiting some distant relatives. When we arrived at their home, we noticed their horse barn. After lunch, our hostess, Fran, offered, "Kathy, would you like to take a horseback ride?"

I swallowed hard. "I haven't been horseback riding for years."

"Oh, you'll do fine. We've got a real gentle horse named Sally."

Within thirty minutes, I was sitting on top of Sally. I gently nudged her ribs and she began to walk. After a few minutes, I felt more comfortable and relaxed. "Hey, this is fun!" I yelled to my mother. Then, all of a sudden, Sally began running. *I don't know how to control a running horse. Help!*

I tried to rein in the speeding horse but couldn't. *Aren't horses supposed to stop when you pull the reins?* I yelled, "Stop! Stop!" Before I knew it, I had lost control. *I can't hold on! I'm going to fall off! Oh, help me, Lord!*

I let go of the reins and as the horse sped forward, as if in slow motion, I felt my body rise high off the horse. Yet, as I fell, I felt light like a feather. As if angels' hands supported my body, I slowly drifted to the ground and landed with a soft thump on my back. My head should have bounced hard against the ground but it didn't.

How strange! I just fell off a running horse and should have at least felt a jolt when I hit the ground. But I didn't! I quickly stood up, embarrassed, and waved my hand at everyone as they watched with mouths agape. "I'm okay!" I called.

It was just two weeks later that I knew the real significance of that floating fall. I didn't know it at that time, but I was pregnant. I rejoiced that God had protected my second child, Mark, and today, he is a handsome, six-foot-one, twenty-three-year-old college senior who is a delight to me.

In His love, God protected that newly created child from destruction and my body from hurt when "my foot slipped." Of course, that doesn't always happen, but God in His sovereign control fulfilled His plan for me and Mark.

I'm so grateful that when we can no longer hold on to situations in life, God, in His love, supports us even more than we realize. If life seems to be slipping out of control or your foot of faith is being jolted out of the stirrups, know that God is supporting.

"Two plus two doesn't equal up to four with God. Two plus two is whatever He says it is—period."
—Wayne Barber

❤ Journal Exercise ❤

In what way do you feel like life is slipping out of control? Tell the Lord how that feels, and then find verses in the Bible that confirm God is firmly in control. Write those references here with a short description of how God is sovereign. —KCM

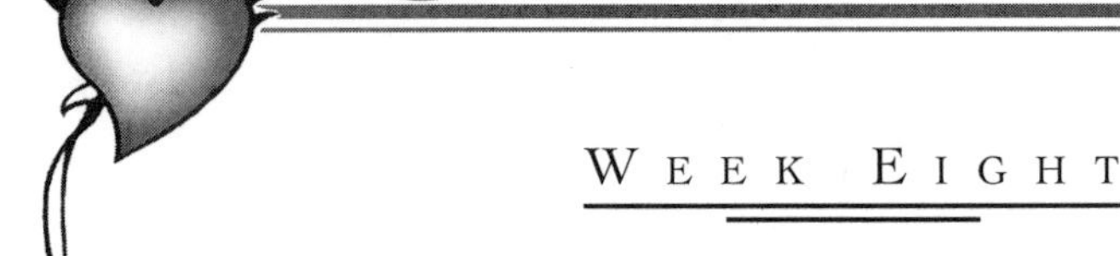

WEEK EIGHT

Don't Forget The Knee-ology

Mary Beth Nelson

Come, let us bow down in worship, let us kneel before the LORD our Maker.
Psalm 95:6

The young minister grinned as he warmly greeted congregation members leaving the Sunday morning service. He had been appointed to the church only three weeks earlier. A well-respected elderly lady stood among those waiting to shake the preacher's hand.

"Young man," probed the wise eighty-one year old, "where did you go to school?"

Slightly straightening his shoulders, he proudly answered her question.

The twinkle in her eye accompanied a friendly wink as she advised, "Well, that's fine, but while you're practicing theology, don't forget to use some knee-ology!"

I never tired of hearing my mother relate this story about the handsome young preacher, my dad. He faithfully exercised this wonderful advice throughout his life. He constantly prayed for wisdom and guidance in God's truth—many times on his knees.

❤ *Lesson* ❤

Using more "knee-ology," or developing a prayer life, is one of the most important things you and I can do. Learning to commune with God and depending on His loving care is the first step towards serenity.

The elements of prayer—acceptance of God's control of the entire universe, acknowledgment of His blessings, and faith in His promises—can only lead to more abundant living.

Someone has said, "The best form of spiritual exercise is to touch the floor regularly with your knees." I cannot think of a better way to worship God than as the Psalmist exhorts us.

Everyone will eventually bow to the Lord God Almighty and acknowledge His sovereignty when they come before Him during eternal judgment. His children ought to be kneeling before Him now.

What's the condition of your knees? You may find that the more they reside on the floor, the more powerfully you live for God.

"I have been driven many times to my knees by the overwhelming conviction that I had nowhere else to go."
—Abraham Lincoln

❤ Journal Exercise ❤

When you picture a subject bowing before a king seated on his throne, what is being communicated in that scene? When you hesitate to bow before the Lord, what do you think you are declaring to God? In that moment, what is preventing you from giving Him the honor He deserves? When you have obeyed anyway, what happened? —KCM

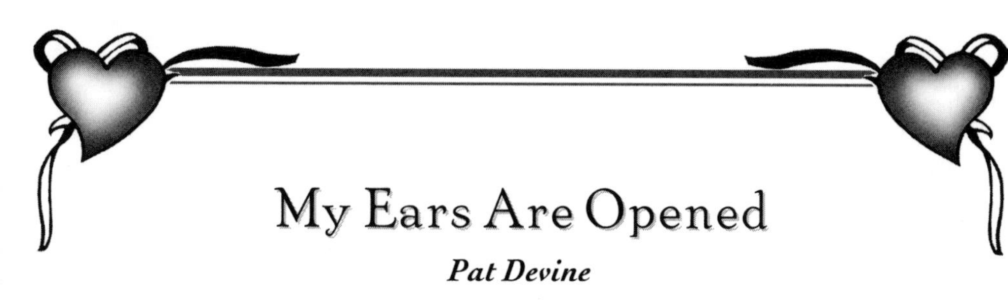

My Ears Are Opened

Pat Devine

Let them sing before the LORD, for he comes to judge the earth.
He will judge the world in righteousness
and the peoples with equity.
Psalm 98:9

Only the obligation I felt to keep my promise to pray sent me off to an hour of prayer and praise in the Adoration Chapel a mile from my home. I drove slowly with the windows open, determined to enjoy the soft autumn air.

As I stopped for a red light, a bouncing black Buick pulled alongside. The driver's braided hair, springing from his head, jiggled to the rhythm of the rap music that blared from his car stereo. He grinned widely and slapped the steering wheel with his open hands to a beat loud enough to penetrate a brick wall.

How can anyone call that *music?*

I was still frowning and fussing over this brief encounter as I entered the foyer of the Adoration Chapel. The sweet aroma of the beeswax candle burning softly in its red glass and the dim interior of the little chapel soothed my frazzled mind. I sat in my favorite chair, breathed deeply, and opened my Bible to Psalm 98. Immediately, memories of peaceful vacations by the sea and mountains filled my mind. I recalled wonder-filled days spent in quiet retreat. I closed my eyes and imagined lyrical harps accompanying a heavenly choir singing sweetly among waving palm trees.

As I repeated the exalted words of Psalm 98, letting them seep into my consciousness, they took on the jarring rap beat I had encountered at the stoplight. Once the beat got into my head I couldn't get rid of it. I tried to return to the soothing sounds of the harp and heavenly choir that my imagination had conjured up, but the raucous rap beat persisted.

I sighed with resignation and let the words speak. I became fascinated with the way the well-loved syllables lent themselves to this (un)musical form I so strongly disliked.

The Psalmist said, "Shout with joy to the Lord; all the earth."

A vision of wiry, lively braids danced before my eyes.

"Let the sea resound, and everything in it, the world, and all who live in it."

Really? Does that include the bouncing Buick and its driver?

I had to agree it could.

❤ Lesson ❤

The God of surprises tore down my walls of prejudice, allowing me to take in all different sounds and use them in praise of Him. I had closed my eyes to the noise and God opened my ears to the hymn of His world.

How often God surprises me! His messages arise in places where I do not expect to find them: in the beat of cacophonous music; in the silence of the gallery as I enjoy the graceful swings of the players in a golf tournament; in the sounds of children kicking tin cans in the street on their way to school; in a baby's cry. I am learning to welcome into my prayer all sounds which break upon my day.

What sounds have you resisted using in praise of God? Could He want to incorporate them into your praise of Him—He who made all sounds?

"What seems to be a waste may lead still to a place
of peace and grace."
—Adrian Van Kaam

❤ Journal Exercise ❤

When did God surprise you recently by showing you His broad pleasure in His world and His created beings? Or maybe He revealed His love for someone that you have a hard time loving or appreciating. What color is your surprise? Yellow? Red? How did this revelation change a small part of your heart or create a difference in your behavior? Or how would you like it to?
—KCM

The Beauty Of Laughter

Jane E. Maxwell

Worship the LORD with gladness; come before him with joyful songs.
Psalm 100:2

A frosty November day chilled my hands as I drove out to the small, white frame house nestled among four tall pine trees. The scent of lavender mingled with antiseptics greeted me as I opened the door.

Emily was adorned in a pair of bright red slacks topped by a flowered red blouse. Her blue eyes twinkled as she adjusted her red wig over her bald head. "Today I'm the daring lady in red," she laughed. Emily's collection of blond and black wigs sat on her dresser, waiting for their turn to be worn on other days.

Emily was in the last stages of cancer after enduring many months of chemotherapy and radiation. Though she had lost much of her strength, weight, and hair, she refused to let cancer rob her of her sense of humor and her joyful songs. I felt privileged to be with her as a hospice volunteer.

When I first began as a hospice volunteer, I was anxious and apprehensive. *Can I really do this? Can I sit and be an empathetic friend to those in the last stages of life without drowning in sorrow myself?* Daily I asked my heavenly Father for wisdom and strength. Gradually, I learned to listen for His joy and embrace life fully on each precious day. Such godly laughter, like prayer, provides hope and a source of strength.

Two years ago the idea of laughter was difficult for me to apply to the care of my terminally ill husband. I was much too serious, intent on trying to fix the symptoms of his illness and control his extreme reactions to chemotherapy and radiation. It became a tense time for both of us. Then, we turned the TV and radio to some of his old favorites — *All in the Family, Andy Griffith,* and *Abbott and Costello,* along with the music he grew up with—and we began to laugh. Tension faded away, pain was lessened, and we reconnected.

❤ *Lesson* ❤

Psalm 100:2 doesn't refer specifically to those who are ill, but every part of our lives is to be filled with worshiping God with joy. Joy demonstrates we're trusting Him and believing He's in charge—even of those about to join Him in heaven. A terminally ill person is much more than his or her disease. Laughter helps us to relate to each other and to remember we are all persons first, still alive and able to enjoy levity.

Maybe you have a friend or loved one who needs the gift of joy and laughter. Prepare your heart to share that gift by reading books such as Courage to Laugh *by Alan Klien,* Laughter Therapy *by Annette Goodheart or* Compassionate Laughter *by Patty Wooten.*

When you are with a friend or loved one who is ill, share funny stories, watch humorous TV shows together, listen to joy-centered tapes, and recall past incidents which were full of fun.

In filling our spirits with joyful thoughts and creating a joyous atmosphere, we will strengthen both those we minister to and our own hearts, too.

"Pain is deeper than all thought; laughter is higher than all pain."
—Elbert Hubbard

❤ Journal Exercise ❤

How does the thought of ministering to a very ill friend or relative make you feel? What do you think would be the most difficult aspect of it? What do you think you could contribute to such a situation? If you've avoided ministering to the ill in the past, what do you think God is saying to you about that now?
—KCM

A Moving Experience

Rose Brandon

**He led them by a straight way to a city where they could settle.
Psalm 107:7**

Moving was out of the question. Our home was located only a block from Doug's office, enabling us to get along with one vehicle. My perennial border in our backyard showed signs of future glory. Above all, we loved our church and friends.

Relocation offered challenging, rewarding employment for Doug. He could live in his favorite place, at the junction of the Great Lakes. An avid fisherman, he wanted to explore the North's rivers.

"Whither thou goest I will go" sounds romantic in a wedding ceremony, but when it came to packing up and following my husband, it felt unfair. So I did what came naturally. I whined. "Why should we move? We've got everything that matters here." What I really meant was, "I have everything that matters to me."

"At least be willing to pray about it," my frustrated husband pleaded. I agreed, believing God would see things my way. But, the more I prayed, the more I saw that relocation wasn't only my husband's idea, it was God's, also.

The company in our new city confirmed its job offer. Our house sold. With a lump in my throat, I buckled our two toddlers into their car seats and made the long journey.

Doug achieved immediate success in commission sales, but it meant working long hours. Even with an eleven-month-old son and three-year-old daughter to care for, I had many quiet hours during their naps and after their bedtime. The phone rarely rang, few visitors called, and we hadn't bothered to hook up the television. Those hours provided time for studying Scripture.

Our home stood at the entrance to the subdivision, like a lighthouse in a busy channel. I prayed for the families in our new neighborhood, specifically praying for a reduction in the divorce rate. Our next door neighbors, known for their volatile relationship, reunited after a ten-month split. They never separated again and are still together today. Soon, the local paper headlined the declining divorce rate in our city. I knew I couldn't have been the only one praying, but I celebrated as if I were.

Brenda, a young Christian woman in the subdivision, became a good friend. Together, we began a women's Bible study. In the months following, many women confessed faith in Jesus Christ. As the group grew, we laid plans for a citywide fellowship of women. Under its umbrella, twelve Bible studies operated in homes across our city.

❤ Lesson ❤

It pained me to move, but I'm glad I did. Following God is always good.

If you're facing the prospect of a new job, new neighborhood or even a new country, think of the change as a holy adventure. God goes ahead of you, as the Psalmist affirms, directing choices and decisions, even those that seem to be controlled by others. He cares where you live and work. Don't be afraid to take His hand and head for parts unknown.

"Without fail He goes before His flock. He knows where to locate the green pastures."
—V. Raymond Edman

❤ Journal Exercise ❤

List all the cities you have lived in. For each one, write down one fear you had of going there. Then list how God met you there. If you weren't yet a believer in Christ, how did God lead you even when you weren't committed to Him? Are you facing any frightening decisions now? How can you apply God's faithfulness in your past moves to your current situation? —KCM

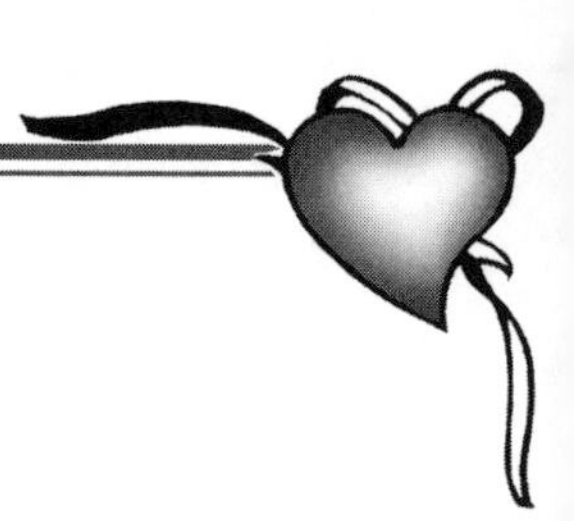

My Delight

Debbie Wong

Great are the works of the LORD; they are pondered by all who delight in them.
Psalm 111:2

In my late twenties, I thought I would be single forever. Prospects seemed scarce. If I met a good-looking, single man at church, I did everything in my power to give him my phone number. But after a few dates, I could tell he wasn't the right guy, or he could tell I wasn't the right girl. So I opened myself up to the world of fix-ups. But even when my friend picked out the "right guy for you," he still wasn't Mr. Right. So, I decided to pull my dance card for a while. I hadn't given up hope, but I realized my choices and my friends' weren't getting me any closer to marriage.

The first few dateless weekends were depressing. A batch of cookie dough, a sappy chick-flick, and a box of tissues were my weekend companions. But after the sulking wore off, I discovered joy in a night alone at home. I often had a date night with God. I would spend those evenings journaling, reading a Christian book, the Bible or renting a thought-provoking movie. I'd talk with God when something in the book or movie stood out to me. I shared my thoughts, feelings, and questions with Him. I grew closer to Him as I talked to Him in the same way I would to anyone I wanted to get to know better. I looked forward to those quiet nights at home. I found such delight in our time together. I still had the desire to be married but I wasn't dwelling on it anymore.

In time, I felt I was ready to reenter the world of dating. But now I had new criteria for the type of guy I would date. Also, I didn't feel a need to go out every weekend since I knew a night at home could be a date night with God. Armed with my renewed relationship with God and a new view of myself, I got back into the dating world.

I consulted God on my choices this time. I still had to kiss a few more frogs before I met my Prince Charming, but eventually God brought him. As I became Mrs. Robert Wong, I realized that because of the time I spent delighting in God, I was able to give Robert the complete Debbie Ullom—the one who knew how to love God with her whole heart and love her husband with her whole heart as well. What a delight!

❤ Lesson ❤

What is your heart's desire? What are you investing your time and energy in? If you have a godly dream that you want to see come true, follow the advice of the Psalmist—"delight yourself in the Lord."

What does that mean? When you delight in a friend or loved one, you enjoy their company. You smile when you reflect on memories of them. Your heart warms as you remember their tenderness in your time of need. God can be that for us, too, if we delight in Him. We'll want to spend time in His Word so that we can know who He truly is.

Once you know Him better, spending time with Him will be a delight. Your eyes will fill with tears when you recall the days that He carried you through terrible crises. Your faith will grow and you'll delight in telling others about His wonderful works in your life. And you'll actually look forward to your date nights with God.

"Till you can sing and rejoice and delight in God, as misers do in gold, and kings in scepters, you never enjoy the world."
—Thomas Traherne

❤ Journal Exercise ❤

We can anticipate our time with God in the same way that we look forward to spending time with a person we love and value. How do you delight in God? Tell God how you feel as you delight in His presence or as you reflect on His incredible love for you. What do you find hinders your delight in Him? How can you counter that? Have you considered that He delights in you? How does that make you feel? —KCM

The End Of All Sorrow

R. C. Sproul

For you, O LORD, have delivered my soul from death, my eyes from tears, my feet from stumbling, that I may walk before the LORD in the land of the living.
Psalm 116:8–9

When I was a child my mother always ministered to me tenderly when I was hurt. When I sobbed with uncontrollable spasms, my mother would take her handkerchief and pat the tears from my cheeks. Often she would "kiss away the tears."

Few human experiences are more intimate than the physical act of wiping away another person's tears. It is a tactile act of compassion. It is a piercing form of nonverbal communication. It is the touch of consolation.

My mother dried my tears more than once. Her consolation worked for the moment, and my sobbing subsided. But then I would get hurt again, and the tears would flow once more. My tear ducts still work. I still have the capacity to weep.

But when God wipes away tears, it is the end of all crying. John writes, "There shall be no more crying." Any tears shed in heaven could only be tears of joy. When God dries our eyes from all sorrowful weeping, the consolation will be permanent.

In heaven there will be no reason for mournful tears. Death will be no more. There will be no sorrow, no pain whatever. These things belong to the former things that shall pass away.

The New Jerusalem has no cemetery, no morgue, no funeral parlor, no hospital, no painkilling drugs. These are the elements that attend the travail of this world. They will all pass away.

❤ *Lesson* ❤

God understands our emotions because Jesus felt those feelings while on earth, but we need not continue our crying all our lives. We can move from grief to joy and from pain to healing—because there is hope through God.

The Psalmist experienced the joy and freedom of seeing God's deliverance. You can have confidence and hope also in God's ability to heal and wipe away those tears. He will patiently bring you through your grief so that you also can exclaim what God has done for you. —KCM

"To believe in heaven is not to run away from life;
it is to run toward it."
—Joseph D. Blinco

❤ Journal Exercise ❤

God says He will wipe away our tears, along with keeping our feet from stumbling. What difference has a knowledge of heaven made to your earthly life? If no difference, why not? How do you think God wants your eternal destiny to have an influence now? What will you do differently because of your heavenly destination? —KCM

Week Nine

Facing Death

Billy Graham

Precious in the sight of the LORD is the death of his saints.
Psalm 116:15

I have faced death many times, and my reactions have not always been the same. One time I had an operation that almost ended me. I knew this could be serious, so before they wheeled me into the operating room I called two of my closest friends and gave them instructions about my wife, my family, and my ministry. Ruth had gone to be with the children, and I tried to keep the seriousness of the situation from her. Whether this was right or wrong, I don't know. At least I'm living to tell the story.

I remember alternating between two feelings. First, the complete peace I had, knowing that I would be with my Lord Jesus Christ, and second, the fear of leaving my loved ones. I certainly thought I was going to die. But the Lord wasn't finished with me.

Death for a Christian is not an accident. The Bible says, "Precious in the sight of the Lord is the death of his saints" (Psalm 116:15 KJV).

How could there be anything precious about death? When a child or a young person dies, the tragedy seems so much greater than for someone who has lived a long life. People begin to question why God would allow such a thing. Do you think that God, whose "eye is on the sparrow" and who knows the very numbers of the hairs on our heads, would turn His back on one of His children in the hour of peril?

❤ *Lesson* ❤

As Billy Graham says, it is difficult to believe that death can be precious. We miss our loved one and that's too painful to consider positively. We understand how God could consider it positively because He receives our loved one into heaven, but from our earthly vantage point, it's not precious at all.

And that's the key. We're looking at it from our inadequate viewpoint. We only know the loss and pain. But God sees the whole picture. If we knew what He knows, we wouldn't be sad at all. Yet, He empathizes that we can't know—all we can do is trust. —KCM

"What is death? For the Christian, death is a friend rather than an enemy. It is another step on the pathway to Heaven rather than a leap into some dark unknown."
—Billy Graham

❤ Journal Exercise ❤

If you've recently experienced the death of a friend or family member, describe your feelings honestly. Are you angry, sad, disappointed, even terrified of being left alone? Write what you think God's saying to you, and open your Bible to find a Scripture that will help to comfort you. Write it here and then write it in your own words as though God is saying it to you personally. —KCM

That I May See Him

Marilyn Krebs

Turn my eyes away from worthless things; preserve my life according to your word.
Psalm 119:37

All morning I'd been busy cleaning house and getting clothes ready in eager anticipation of our upcoming vacation. By lunchtime I decided to relax and watch an old movie, a love story. From the title it sounded like one I'd enjoy. However, as the drama unfolded I considered turning it off because, though it had passion and romance, it was also packed with frustration, despair, and heartbreak. But, incurable romantic that I am, I watched it to the end and ended up depressed. When my husband came home from work an hour later, I snapped at him.

"What's wrong with you?" he asked, bewildered.

By bedtime I was asking myself the same question, *What's wrong with you? You could have avoided all this stress.*

The following morning I was able to explain to him that I'd gotten involved in watching a movie and had refused to listen to my conscience. That had opened the door to a turmoil of negative emotions, allowing them to influence my thinking. After my apology, life returned to normal.

❤ *Lesson* ❤

I learned a significant lesson. I need to use caution in what I let my eyes take in, because the things I view will affect my thinking, and ultimately my actions. If I'm not focusing on things that are informative, uplifting, and wholesome, I will be affected negatively, and my actions will prove it.

The advertising profession is notorious for knowing how to attract consumers. I can't control the media, but I can keep my eyes away from the world's offering of entertainment and advertisements, which are designed to create discontent. For instance, when I'm standing in the checkout line at the grocery store, I have to exercise my will and drag my eyes away from the headlines of the gossip sheets. I have an active imagination, and if I ignore my judgment of what is good and wholesome, my conscience will soon become dulled.

Our sight is a wonderful gift—just ask someone who has lost theirs. We must not abuse it. Yet, it takes discipline and courage to do what is right. There is no magical way of eliminating the visual pollution in the world, but we can take responsibility for our eyes.

The Psalmist made a commitment in Psalm 119:37 to turn his eyes away from worthless things. He knew that doing so would keep him faithful to the Lord and living the way God wanted him to live.

If you want to grow in your walk with God, and reap the benefits and blessings He has for you, then you must take seriously what you put before your eyes. Focusing on things that defile and invite compromise will bring destruction. Seeking to look upon things that uplift and nourish the soul will give you the vigorous life and spiritual health God has promised.

"In a situation that looks like trouble, never take a second look, and never cross the line."

—Unknown

❤ Journal Exercise ❤

What do you find most attractive in the world's offerings that actually diminish your spiritual health? Why do those things seem necessary? What could you replace them with? If you focused instead on things that fed your spirit and walk with Christ, how would your life be changed? What one thing could you choose to do differently today? —KCM

Takin' Life To The Hoop

Sharon Norris

This has been my practice: I obey your precepts.
Psalm 119:56

My current interest in the game of basketball began on a slightly lower plateau than the NBA, college ball, or even the high school team at the school where I teach. When my youngest son, Mark, was five years old, he played in a junior YMCA league. Both Mark and I learned about the game from the ground up. A typical practice went something like this:

First, the team warmed up. They performed various stretching exercises and ran a couple of laps around the gym.

Then they did drills. They practiced rudimentary skills such as dribbling and passing.

Then it was time to practice shooting. They learned to shoot from all different positions on the court.

Finally, the coach divided the team in half and they played the game. All the while, the coach was speaking "basketball-ese" to them. They heard and responded to words like rebound, block, foul, free throw, double-team, back court press, offense, and defense. The boys excitedly raced up and down the court, trying to do everything they had been taught, spotting their teammates and yelling, "I'm open!"

Basketball is so much like the Christian life.

As we become exposed to Christianity, it will all seem very strange at first. We have to warm up to the idea that a personal, loving God, personally loves us. We soon stretch out enough to confess our sins, receive forgiveness, and begin running laps from home to school to church.

But just when we become used to that routine, God starts taking us through drills. We know the Bible teaches that stealing is wrong, then we enter a store with no salesperson present. We learn to honor our parents, then they get on our last nerve. We read about fleeing fornication, then we fall in love. As these things face us, the Coach lets us know it's time to practice shooting. We must stand at the line and work on "shooting" down the temptations that come at us from anywhere on the "court."

Although sometimes it gets frustrating and we don't always make the shots or get the rebounds, before we even realize it, we're in the full court game of living this Christian life. And all the while, because we continue to plug along day to day, we have been learning to hear and respond to "Christian-ese." We find ourselves adding skills like forgiveness, love, joy, peace, and patience, to our game-playing style. It becomes exciting to realize that, yes, we are a part of the team and our Coach has no intention of leaving us sitting on the bench away from the action. Once we settle into the rhythm of the "game," we can put all of our skills into play, spot our teammate Jesus and yell, "I'm open!"

As stated by the Psalmist in Psalm 119:56, make it your "practice" to hear and obey the voice of God. With Him as your coach in the game of life, it is impossible to be defeated.

"Practice yourself, for heaven's sake, in little things;
and thence proceed to greater."
—Epictetus

❤ Journal Exercise ❤

What "drills" has God been encouraging you to practice—prayer, Bible study, fellowship with other Christians? Have you been sitting on the sidelines instead of participating in the game? Are you obeying the Coach's instructions? Write out a commitment in obedience to what God is calling you to do. —KCM

Thanks, I Needed That!

Karen Davis

It was good for me to be afflicted so that I might learn your decrees.
Psalm 119:71

Right after high school, I moved to southern California to begin my first year of college. Life was very exciting. The college students at my new church went skating every Monday night for fellowship and fun. I looked forward to my Monday nights. I would take a bus to the rink around four o'clock in the afternoon, finishing up my homework during the ride.

One Monday, I heard an inner voice say, "Don't go skating today."

I ignored the nudge and continued with my normal Monday afternoon schedule. As the time approached for me to catch my bus, the voice became stronger, "Don't go tonight!"

This was really starting to annoy me. I thought, *There is no reason I shouldn't go and I want to go, so I'm going.*

I left my dorm, walked the half mile to the bus stop and waited. Thirty minutes passed and no bus. This was the first time since I had starting taking the Monday afternoon bus that it was late.

If the bus doesn't come soon, I thought, *I'll miss the connecting bus*. As I reviewed the schedule, the bus rounded the corner on the opposite side of the street. As it came into full view, I saw that it was completely full of junior high school kids, so full the driver did not even stop. He slowed down long enough to make a hand gesture indicating that another bus was coming right behind him. As the bus pulled away from the curb, a boy stuck his head out of the window and spit. To my horrible dismay, the spittle landed on my left cheek.

Thoroughly humiliated, I immediately turned around, wiped my face, and walked back very quickly to my dorm room. I washed my face, closed the blinds, and plopped myself down on my bed. As I stared at the ceiling feeling angry and embarrassed, I heard the voice of the Lord say, "I want you to pray."

I reluctantly slid off the bed onto my knees but in my heart I was throwing a tantrum. I started to say, "I don't have anything to say" and was interrupted with, *"I have something to say to you. You are walking in rebellion and I want you to stop. I did not bring you to southern California so that you could attend school and have fun skating. I have a call on your life and you must learn how to listen to My voice and obey."*

Overcome with conviction, I wept and repented of the secret rebellion in my heart.

❤ *Lesson* ❤

To this day I thank God for that experience and the many other ones that He has used to bring me to a place of obedience. In the beginning, I was afraid to let go of my hopes and desires. But in God's school of obedience, I have learned the joy of yielding to Him. The Psalmist was right. It is good to be corrected and disciplined by the Lord so that we will learn His "decrees"—the way He wants us to walk in obedience to Him.

Because I've learned to yield to His plans, I now know God has my best interests at heart.

Do you know God has your best interests at heart—even when He corrects and disciplines you?

"Trust and obey, there is no other way to live happy with Jesus than to trust and obey."

—Old hymn

❤ Journal Exercise ❤

Do you try to avoid God's correction or do you welcome it? Write down how you feel when you know the Lord is disciplining you. Do you ever feel loved like a child who is so valuable that his Father is steering him in the right direction? What do you need to change in your thinking in order to get to that point? —KCM

No Comparison

Vivian Lee Baniak

Your hands have made me and fashioned me. Give me understanding that I may learn Your commandments.
Psalm 119:73

The house was dark and quiet, but I couldn't get to sleep. Creeping out of bed in the 2:00 A.M. darkness, I fumbled for my slippers and robe. As I groped my way toward the kitchen, I decided to brew a cup of hot tea and read for awhile until I felt sleepy again. I settled down on the family room sofa with my steaming cup and picked up a book by a well-known Christian author.

Instead of reading, I found myself contemplating the ministry of the author/speaker. I admired her greatly. I thought about the ministry that God had given to her and that He had not given to me. Suddenly, I recognized that I did not simply admire this woman; I was jealous of her!

"O Lord, I confess my envy. Please forgive me," I blurted out. "I must stop comparing myself with others. Instead I will focus on what I do have and who I am in You."

I put down the book and closed my eyes. A picture of white lace, delicate and fine like handmade Belgian lace, came to my mind. The Lord spoke comfort softly to my heart. "See this lace," He seemed to say. "Look at it carefully."

He called my attention away from the pattern to the holes. "Notice the holes. They are just as important as the threads. They make up the pattern of the lace and are just as much a part of it as the rest.

"Your life is like this lace. What I have put in it and what I have left out are both of value in creating the overall effect of your life. When you see what you think is a hole, remember that I am the one who fashioned you. There is nothing that I intended for you to have that you do not have. I have fashioned the design for your life that makes you uniquely suited for My plan for you."

"O Father, I see now. Teach me to appreciate the lace of my life, both the thread and the holes. I praise You for You are the great lace maker and You never make a mistake."

Do you struggle with comparing yourself to others as I do? Do feelings of inadequacy sometimes overwhelm you? This battle of comparisons and jealousy is waged in your thought life. The victory comes in replacing lies you may have heard about yourself all your life with the truth of God's Word.

Replace those lies with the truth that your unique design in God's overall plan is absolutely perfect—and it's accomplished through both the threads and the holes of the lace of your life. Psalm 119:73 promises that God took personal interest in your formation and created you for His purposes. And He wants you to know what those purposes are. By focusing on His wonderful design for you, you'll fill your mind with His truth and comparing yourself to others will have no stronghold over you.

"You can't unveil truth when you like; when the unveiling comes, beware. That moment marks your going back or your going on."
—Oswald Chambers

❤ Journal Exercise ❤

Do you focus more on the threads or the holes in the lace of your life? How has God used the spaces in the fabric of your being? Make a list of the things you like about yourself here. Then on a separate piece of paper make another list of the things you don't like about yourself. In a ceremony of surrender, burn that separate piece of paper and refuse to compare yourself to anyone else. —KCM

An Encouraging Word

Charles Stanley

Your promises have been thoroughly tested,
and your servant loves them.
Psalm 119:140

In the margin next to many Scripture verses in my Bible are clearly marked dates. Each one indicates an instance when God spoke to me through the verse to encourage me in times of testing or adversity. I cannot tell you how many times a Bible promise has sustained me in difficult straits. It is light in darkness, strength in weakness, and nourishing manna for my soul.

A Bible promise is God's Word of encouragement for you to claim by faith and cling to in rough waters. When a battered Paul was hesitant to stay in Corinth, God promised him safekeeping (Acts 18:9–10). When the ship that was transferring him to Rome was about to sink, God sent an angel to Paul to declare that he would stand before Caesar and the lives of all those aboard would be spared (Acts 27:23–24). When Joshua prepared to enter the Promised Land, God encouraged him with the assurance of His presence and deliverance from the land's inhabitants (Joshua 1:29).

❤ *Lesson* ❤

A Bible promise from God is a declaration of His intention to graciously bestow a gift upon His children. Some promises are conditional, fulfilled only upon the believer's obedience to a clearly stated condition. For example, if you want to experience God's best financially, you must first give of your resources. Other promises have specific limitations, such as God's covenant promise to Abraham that he would become the father of many nations. But there are many promises God desires to see claimed and appropriated in our lives that require only trust in Him.

God's promises usually meet a specific need in your life. You may be reading the Scriptures, and a verse becomes divinely highlighted by the Holy Spirit. This is a promise from God you may claim if you do not take it out of context (manipulate it to apply to an irrelevant situation), and if your interpretation of it does not contradict any other portion of Scripture. The Spirit of God witnesses to your spirit that it is from God, and the ultimate purpose is to glorify Him.

When God speaks to you in such a way, you have a promise that will anchor your mind, will, and emotion. You can meditate on it day and night, standing on the authority and power of the Word of God. It becomes part of your being.

God's promises have never let me down. God cannot lie. If you will discipline yourself to read His Word consistently and obediently and wait patiently and submissively for Him to fulfill His promises, you will discover truth you can stand on in any weather. Nothing promotes peace like God's encouraging Word.

"A Bible promise is God's guaranteed means of encouragement."
—Charles Stanley

❤ Journal Exercise ❤

God's promises are comforting, encouraging and strengthening. What is your favorite promise in the Bible? Why? Describe how God used it in the past to comfort, encourage or strengthen you. Who do you know who needs to hear God's promise today? Communicate it to them. —KCM

WEEK TEN

Divine Appointment

Elizabeth Hey

The LORD will keep you from all harm—he will watch over your life; the LORD will watch over your coming and going both now and forevermore.
Psalm 121:7–8

I exited the plane and walked quickly through the maze of people to the taxi stand. Ironically, this was the moment I dreaded most. Home from my first business trip, I scanned the curb for a taxi. I felt alone and vulnerable relying on a stranger to deliver me to my friend's isolated farm, where no one would be home. I decided to face my fear and trust the Lord.

I spotted a taxi near the end of the queue. Opening the door, I leaned over and peered inside. The driver glanced over his shoulder at me and smiled. I climbed in, plunked my carry-on beside me, and recited the address to the large, middle-aged driver. He seemed pleasant. *Maybe this won't be so bad after all,* I decided. Preparing to endure the ride, I glanced at the taxi's dashboard. Perched directly under the rearview mirror was a large, well-worn Bible. Surprised and reassured, I settled back to enjoy the ride.

Twenty minutes passed quickly as the driver and I talked about our faith and our Lord. At the farm, I reached into my billfold to pay him. Stretching over the seat, he handed me his business card, and I slipped it into my purse. I pulled my luggage across the seat, opened the door, and stepped out into the quiet of late afternoon.

Today, my billfold still carries the taxi driver's business card. Printed in capitals, it reminds me—"MY FATHER MAKES ALL MY APPOINTMENTS. Terminal Cab #392 & #393. GOD only makes us to dwell in safety."

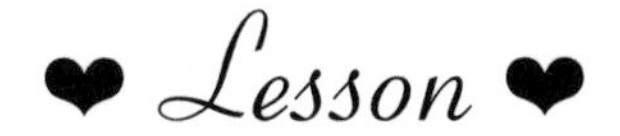

No fear or concern is insignificant to the Lord. I am thankful that life's smallest details are important to the One who has numbered the hairs on my head. Sometimes we wonder if God is truly sovereign in this crazy world, but He is. Developing our own personal history of His faithfulness toward us increases our ability to trust Him when fearful times arise.

In ancient times, the people of Israel erected altars as reminders of God's intervention in their lives. Today, memorials of the Lord's faithfulness aren't usually made of stone, but when God hands us His business card—in creative ways—we celebrate, just as the Psalmist did. In that moment, confidence in His goodness spreads through our hearts, building our faith.

When worries and fears threaten us, we can remember that God Himself appoints our coming and going.

"Faith expects from God what is beyond all expectation."
—Andrew Murray

❤ Journal Exercise ❤

When did God protect you? How did that increase your faith and trust in Him? Has there been a time when it seemed as though He didn't protect you? How does that go along with the promise of this verse? Life isn't guaranteed to be free from hard times, so what would you share with someone who has doubts about God's protection? —KCM

Faith Outside The Box

Christa Weisser

As the eyes of slaves look to the hand of their master, as the eyes of a maid look to the hand of her mistress, so our eyes look to the LORD our God, till he shows us his mercy.
Psalm 123:2

"Where in the world did I put that?" In the middle of packing up my last boxes for the moving company, I realized that I had misplaced one hundred dollars. The money was safely secure in an envelope . . . somewhere.

My move to Florida was an answer to prayer. I had been looking for a job like this for months. I did not have a place to live yet, but I knew that God would work everything out. He had given me the job and was not going to leave me homeless. I had grown a lot in my faith over the last few months, while all of the last details for the job were being worked out. I felt that way, that is, until this moment.

"I can't find the money anywhere. I really can't afford to lose that much money right now, but it's gone," I moaned as I slumped onto my bed.

"It'll show up in a place that you have probably overlooked," my sister responded, trying to comfort me.

At that moment, I remembered that I had had enough faith to trust God about finding a job. I had faith about moving somewhere without an address to call home. But for the simple faith that God would help me to find the money, I was at a loss.

"I have a boxed up faith," I mumbled. "I have faith in God except for the things that are more than I can handle." Then I realized, "I can't handle anything without God."

❤ Lesson ❤

Committing everything to the Lord is often easier during the great storms of our lives because our need is so great. But trusting God for the little, everyday moments of frustration or anxiety often seems unnecessary. We often stop trusting God because we think that we are facing something we can handle. We tell the God of the universe, "I got this one," if not through our words, then through our actions. But committing everything to Him means just that: committing everything!

Is there a place at which your faith wavers? The same faith that will remove the mountain from in front of you will remove the pebble from your shoe. The same trust in God to provide me with a job led me to find the lost hundred dollars in a place I had already searched four times.

What are you facing at this moment? A sick family member? A broken relationship? A project that erased from your computer? A lost button that fell off your favorite shirt? How much faith do you have in God to help you through?

The Psalmist wrote that just as the maid looks to her mistress for everything, we should look to our great God for everything. What will happen when you commit everything to the Lord and trust Him? Do not expect Him to help you in the exact way you planned, or at your appointed time. The answer may be in a place where you have looked before.

Do not put God in a box. For we really get to know and trust God when we view Him as He is outside of the boxed ideas.

"Although you think it is yourself you are doubting,
you are really doubting the Lord."
—Hannah Whitall Smith

❤ Journal Exercise ❤

How big is your God? Describe your God and evaluate how much of your life you think He's really interested in. Can you think of a recent time when you neglected to include Him on some small issue? Did He show you He wanted to be part of it? What small thing would He like to be involved in right now? —KCM

Laugh Again!

Charles Swindoll

When the LORD brought back the captives to Zion, we were like men who dreamed. Our mouths were filled with laughter, our tongues with songs of joy. Then it was said among the nations, "The LORD has done great things for them."
Psalm 126:1–2

My vocation is among the most serious of all professions. As a minister of the gospel and as the senior pastor of a church, the concerns I deal with are eternal in dimension. A week doesn't pass without my hearing of or dealing with life in the raw. Marriages are breaking, homes are splitting, people are hurting, jobs are dissolving, addictions of every description are rampant. Needs are enormous, endless, and heartrending.

The most natural thing for me to do would be to allow all of that to rob me of my joy and to change me from a person who has always found humor in life—as well as laughed loudly and often—into a stoic, frowning clergyman. No thanks.

Matter of fact, that was my number-one fear many years ago. Thinking that I must look somber and be ultraserious twenty-four hours a day resulted in my resisting a call into the ministry for several years. Most of the men of the cloth I had seen looked like they held down a night job at the local mortuary. I distinctly remember wrestling with the Lord over all this before He pinned me to the mat and whispered a promise in my ear that forced me to surrender: "You can faithfully serve Me, but you can still be yourself. Being My servant doesn't require you to stop laughing." That did it. That one statement won me over. I finally decided I could be one of God's spokesmen and still enjoy life.

❤ *Lesson* ❤

Not too many years ago when I started the radio program, Insight for Living, *I flashed back to that original call, and I decided to be myself, no matter what. Whether the broadcasts succeeded or fizzled, I wasn't about to come across as some super-pious religious fanatic, intense about everything. When things struck me funny, I would laugh.*

One of the listeners wrote in and commented: "I appreciate your program. The teaching has helped a lot . . . but I have one major request: Don't stop laughing! You can stop teaching and you can make whatever other changes you wish on your broadcasts, but **don't stop laughing!**" *And then she added: "Yours is the only laughter that comes into our home."*

Her ten concluding words have been ringing in my ears for years. What a sad commentary on our times! In many homes—dare I say most?—laughter has left. Joy that was once a vital ingredient in family life has departed, leaving hearts that seldom sing, lips that rarely smile, eyes that no longer dance, and faces that say no. Tragically, this is true in Christian homes as well as non-Christian . . . maybe more so.

It is my firm conviction that a change is urgently needed.

"Only if we are secure in our beliefs can we see
the comical side of the universure."
—Flannery O'Connor

❤ Journal Exercise ❤

When you find yourself too solemn, what has usually happened? What stress factor creates solemnity in you? At that point, what helps to restore your joy? Do you think there's a difference between laughter and joy? If so, what is it? If they are different, how can you choose joy and include laughter? —KCM

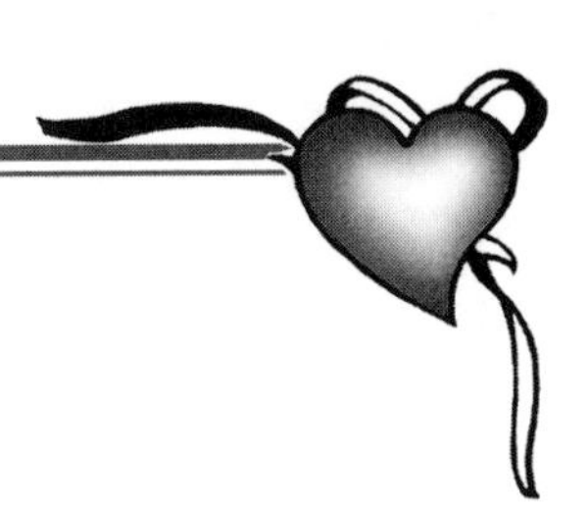

"Wake Up!"

Les Enloe

Sons are a heritage from the LORD,
children a reward from Him.
Psalm 127:3

I'd been looking forward to sleeping in that Saturday morning. When you have four children, "sleeping in" usually means being allowed to sleep (or at least keep your eyes closed) till maybe 7:30. At about 6:40 A.M., five-year-old Matthew crept quietly in.

"Are you awake, Dad?" he whispered about four inches from my face.

I tried to ignore him.

"Dad," he got a little louder, "Are you awake?"

I thought about answering, "No," but thought better of it. I cocked my eye half open. "What is it, Matty?"

"I just wanted to know if you were awake. Can I get in?"

A dozen responses ambled through my head, but the Lord was gracious enough to keep my mouth closed. As I lifted the comforter, Matthew crawled in and snuggled up close. I struggled to hold on to just a few more moments of sleep, but they eluded me. I was awake. *I may never be able to sleep in again. Ever,* I thought.

Later in the day I realized: yes, someday I will be able to sleep in again. In all-too-few years, I'll be able to sleep in *every* weekend. All four of my children will be grown, and they'll probably be gone. They won't even remember getting up at 6:40, let alone crawling into my bed on a Saturday morning.

But I will. And I'll miss it dearly. It's already happening. My nine year old, Christopher—who used to crawl in all the time—doesn't do it anymore. And neither does Jacqueline ("Dad, a twelve year old would *never* do that!"). Our two year old, Stephen, sleeps with us quite a bit, but when will he be out?

During the ensuing week, I thought about how fleeting childhood is and what a blessing it is to enjoy it with my children. These precious moments are here, and then they're gone, like a vapor. How much longer will I be able to enjoy them telling me about their imaginary friends? Or asking for the seventh "just one more" glass of water? ("This is the last, last, last one, Dad! Honest!")

As the weekend approached, I dreaded the idea of sleeping in. I wanted to be with my children. It didn't matter that they don't realize how precious it is.

Saturday morning came, and 6:40 rolled around. 6:41. 6:42. At 6:43, Matty came in. A little while later, Christopher joined us. Then Jacqueline. And, with a smile that none of them knew the cause of, I silently rejoiced in the Lord over my children.

❤ Lesson ❤

The Psalmist reminds us that children are a gift from the Lord. Yet, they are not ours to keep. They're on loan. As with time, money, and any other blessings from the Lord, we are stewards. Parenthood is such an important stewardship God entrusts us with, as children are so precious to Him.

They're ours to guide, protect, teach, encourage, and even, at times, to discipline—all in God's love. And we need to be grateful—even if they keep us from sleeping in. They're worth it.

"When these parenting years have passed, something precious will have flickered and gone out of my life. Thus, I am resolved to enjoy every day that remains in this fathering era."
—Dr. James Dobson

❤ Journal Exercise ❤

In one column, write out the things you don't like about being a parent. In a second column, the things you do appreciate. How important are the "negative" aspects? Is it possible you might "miss" some of those things when they're gone? Write down a blessing that you want to say to your children, regardless of their age. —KCM

Forgiven Beyond My Wildest Dreams

Charles R. Brown

If You, O LORD, kept a record of sins, O LORD, who could stand it? But with You there is forgiveness; therefore You are feared.
Psalm 130:3–4

They had come to begin a Bible study with me. It was to be a time of growing and learning together. But other matters of the heart cried for discussion, matters that caused them to sit closely with hands pressed together for courage to overcome their fear.

Weeping uncontrollably, my seventeen-year-old daughter tried to share her burden but couldn't.

My wife, Bobbie, spoke up, "Honey, what is it? You know we love you. Tell us!"

My daughter and her boyfriend looked at each other, and finally my daughter controlled her sobs enough to speak, "I'm pregnant." Then she broke into fresh tears.

She regained enough composure to mumble, "Mom, Dad, we're sorry. So very sorry! Please forgive us!"

I stared at the floor as I tried to dislodge the words tangled in my throat. I groaned. What should I say? What should I do? Violent colors of emotion raced across my mind. And yet, as we sat together in our living room with this unplanned agenda, God's love bathed me as the Prince of Peace embraced us.

"This is difficult," I choked out. "But, hearing your confession and sorrow makes a big difference. It's times like this that I'm reminded of God's wide open arms that have been extended to me.

He has forgiven me over and over and over. I must forgive you if I am to be like my Forgiver."

That step of forgiveness was God's first footprint in the healing of our family. They married and blessed us with our most precious grandson.

Who could stand me if I continually pointed out the failings of my friends and family? What child would want to be around me if I were the type of person who reminded him or her of past mistakes and sins? Which coworkers would want to have lunch with me if I had the reputation of bringing up old errors and embarrassments?

The God of all creation, the God who knows everything, somehow has the ability to forgive and forget. The Psalmist says if God kept a record of my sins I would not be able to stand. I would be flattened by my guilt, pinned to the ground because of my disobedience. "But," says the Book, with God, "there is forgiveness."

We love because He first loved us. And we can forgive because He first forgave us.

The Psalmist reminds us that God doesn't keep a record of our forgiven sins—and neither should we. Each day we must burn that little notebook filled with "sins of the saints" that we could be tempted to review.

What step of forgiveness do you need to take?

"Confession is not only about the stupid stuff we did yesterday,
it is also about the magnificent stuff God did
while we were yet sinners."
—Robert Benson

❤ Journal Exercise ❤

Forgiving others, especially if they've hurt us, may be the most difficult thing we ever do. Yet, it's when we forgive that we are most like God. Who comes to mind that needs your forgiveness? On a separate piece of paper, write down what he/she did to you and then burn it in a forgiveness ceremony. If it's appropriate, write here a note of forgiveness, and then send it to that person if the Lord leads. —KCM

Second Choice

Jan Coleman

I wait for the LORD, my soul waits and in his word
I put my hope.
Psalm 130:5

As I left the office, a huge sigh of pleasure escaped me. The job interview had gone better than I had expected. The elevator gracefully opened as if to congratulate me. The job was mine. I just knew it!

I needed a job. My hope and money were running out. Six months before, my husband had left me and our two young daughters for someone else. I had drooped around for months praying he'd come back to us, but I finally realized that I was on my own. I had no choice but to pull myself together and go to work for the first time in fifteen years.

I really wanted to be a writer, but how could I support a family with freelance work? I knew God would get us through, but wasn't He dragging His feet?

But I didn't panic. I took a couple of computer classes and spiffed up my resume. One day, while scouring the want ads, I found one for a secretary with writing skills. I eagerly sent off a letter and shrieked with joy when I was called to a state senator's district office for an interview.

As I sat across from the chief aide, my ears perked up at the job description—writing and dealing with the public. This position was tailor-made for my skills and personality. For the first time since my husband left, I saw a glimmer of hope for my future.

When the official-looking letter came a week later I ripped it open. "*While the decision was a difficult one . . .*" I read it again just to be sure. The job went to someone else? I made a strong showing, and I was the *second* choice. The winning candidate had legislative experience. She had a slight edge.

Where was *my* slight edge? I had no backup job offers, and we were down to our last few dollars. I'd been certain this job was from God. How could I have been so wrong? That night I wrestled with the Lord. *Why? Why can't You bring my husband home? Why must I leave my young children and go to work? Why can't the only job I want be mine?*

Two weeks later, I had a message to call the Senator's office. I clenched my teeth as I anxiously dialed the phone. I vaguely heard something about an authorization paperwork jam at the state level. The number one choice couldn't wait. Was there a chance I was still available?

❤ Lesson ❤

The night I wrestled with God I died to some of my dreams, including the perfect job. If the job had been mine right away, I may have missed the lesson; that He was less interested in what I am to "do" than who I am to "be." I may have been the second choice, but God had the last word. And I am "first" with Him.

The Psalmist tells us the attitude we're to have in times of waiting: put our hope in a wonderful God who wants only the best for us. When your hopes are dark, it means they are being refined, shaped for His purposes, and always for your good. Just hang on with certainty that He is full of surprises. He will plant you where He chooses in just the right time and place.

"Never think that God's delays are God's denials.
Hold on; hold fast; hold out."
—Louis Leclerc de Buffon

❤ Journal Exercise ❤

When you are waiting for God's answer, how does your body feel? What are your thoughts? How does your waiting express itself? What was the longest you had to wait for God to work in a situation? How was your "hope" level? What would you tell someone whose hope is nearly depleted as they wait for God's provision? —KCM

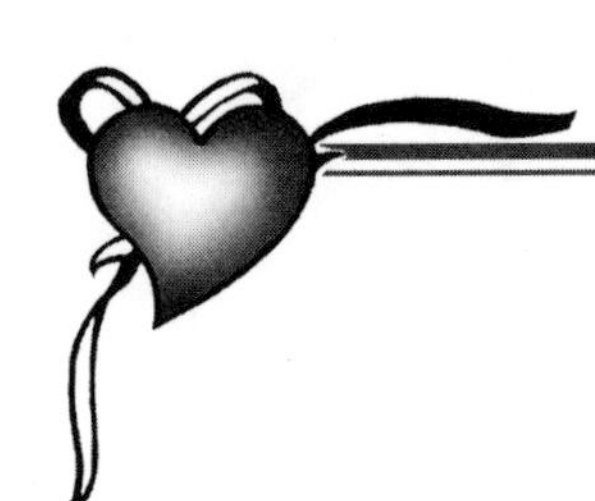

WEEK ELEVEN

Sitting In Traffic

Kelly Bell

My soul waits for the LORD more than watchmen wait for the morning, more than watchmen wait for the morning. O Israel, put your hope in the LORD, for with the LORD is unfailing love and with Him is full redemption.
Psalm 130:6–7

Sitting in traffic. I hate it. Of course, it only happens when I'm either late or in a hurry! Recently I sat on the 15 Freeway for what seemed like an eternity—four hours to be exact. It started with the dreaded sign right before I reached the mall—"Accident." They were nice enough to put a detour sign off to one side, but whenever I take a detour, I wind up getting lost, and reaching my destination even later! So there I sat. I was a caretaker for my mother and she needed her medicine at the proper time. Of course, I didn't have my car phone to call her neighbor. I simply could not afford to be late that day. But that doesn't matter when you're in a traffic jam.

By the time I arrived at my mother's home, the Lord had already been there and taken care of everything. He had sent a nurse over for an "unexpected" visit and she was able to give my mother the medicine she so badly needed.

Again, I was taught the valuable lesson of waiting on the Lord. He is in control of every detail of my life, so why panic? I am so thankful that even when I have to sit in a traffic jam, God doesn't. Nothing can stand in the way of His will.

❤ *Lesson* ❤

Sometimes, the trials and storms in our Christian life are like sitting in a traffic jam. When we are forced to wait, we become anxious. We don't understand why it has to take so long! We want to be finished with the trial or the disagreement or the uncertainty.

Unfortunately, we don't know how long we will sit and wait in a traffic jam, or be in the middle of our trials. But we do know this. They always pass eventually! There's always an end. The Lord is there to give us the strength and patience we need to get through them. We can choose to be frustrated, angry, and miserable . . . or we can sit back, relax, and wait patiently. Our loving heavenly Father wants to mold us and shape us through every trial we face. Waiting on the Lord strengthens our heart and builds our faith, as well as shaping our character.

Are you sitting in a "spiritual traffic jam?" Has God put you in a position where all you can do is wait? Call out to the Lord with the Psalmist and know that He hears you. Choose to fight the temptation to become frustrated and instead "hope" in a God who cares about every detail of your life. Instead of striving against His training in patience, cooperate! Allow your faith to be strengthened, and take heart! God is right on time!

"Listen to the Lord. If you do not hear His voice at once, then wait patiently. He is a Good Shepherd, and a good shepherd talks to His sheep. Waiting on the Lord is a blessing in itself. Do not immediately put down the receiver. He loves you, and He longs to say many things to you!"
—Corrie ten Boom

❤ Journal Exercise ❤

How do you feel about God as you wait? What do you think He would say to you right now if you had a personal audience with Him? Can you think of a time in the past when waiting produced a much better result than you had expected? What growth in your character was accomplished? How can that help you to wait more patiently right now? —KCM

Just You

Heather Harlan Bacus

But I have stilled and quieted my soul; like a weaned child with its mother, like a weaned child is my soul within me.
Psalm 131:2

"Mommy!"

I tried to ignore the little voice.

"Moommmmmeeeee!"

I just want to finish doing the dishes, I thought.

Too late. I felt a tug on the back pockets of my jeans.

Raising six-year-old Micah, our son, and four-year-old Robin, our daughter, was a wonder-filled experience, but the constant interruptions that came with the job title "stay-at-home mom" proved a challenge. Finishing basic cleaning tasks seemed impossible, and my nerves were fraying.

When they were nursing as babies, life was actually a little easier. True, they wanted and needed something from me on a regular basis, but since their most urgent needs were for milk and attention, I reveled in the fact that nursing satisfied both. Now, satisfying them wasn't quite as simple.

"Probably wants a snack or a drink. Not another game of Candyland. I do *not* have time," I muttered.

"Mommmmmeeeee!" Robin cried again as she stood by my side.

"*What?*" I barked as I banged my sudsy fist on the counter.

Her mouth quivered, and her eyes brimmed with tears.

"You," she whispered. "I just wanted you."

"I-I-I'm sorry, honey," I stammered. I scooped her up with my wet hands and we headed for the oak rocking chair. Robin nestled in my lap, wisps of her blonde hair tickling my chin. After a few minutes of silent rocking, she hugged my neck, I pecked her on the cheek, and she skipped off to find her brother.

She wasn't a nursing baby anymore, and she didn't want to eat, or play a game. She didn't want anything *from* me. My daughter just wanted *me*!

❤ *Lesson* ❤

Often I approach God with the mind-set that I want something from Him, even if the "things" are "Christian." I draw near to His throne with a spiritual laundry list to grasp joy, guidance, or even His will.

When I was seventeen years old, my journey as a Christian began when a counselor at church camp remarked, "Christianity is not a religion; it is a relationship." Music, church life, prayer, and study of the Scriptures are tools to cultivate that relationship. But am I learning to sit on His lap and be content with His presence?

The Psalmist refers to a weaned child's contentment. The child doesn't want milk from his mother, but her presence. The root of the word "wean" is to be satisfied.

Are you growing and learning, as a weaned child does, just to be content with the presence of the loving parent? Can you be satisfied without any thing*—only Him?*

If He were to ask you, "What do you want, My Child?" could you still and quiet your soul like a weaned child and answer, "You, Father. I just want You"?

"Don't wrestle. Just nestle."
—Corrie ten Boom

❤ Journal Exercise ❤

Do you commonly sit in the Lord's presence during your quiet times without asking for anything? How do you fellowship with Him during that time? If you were to explain that experience to someone else, what would you say? How does it make you feel to know God enjoys your attention? Write down what you think He's saying to you right now as you sit in His presence. —KCM

Making Harmony

Muriel Larson

How good and pleasant it is when brothers live together in unity!
Psalm 133:1

Our children's Sunday school assembly time had ended and I had dismissed the children to their classes. The singing time had been a near disaster. Three out of four times I'd gotten the starting note wrong and had been embarrassed. After I dismissed the children that day, I said to the fourteen-year-old pianist, "I'm sorry, Chris, but I just couldn't seem to get the starting notes today!"

She snapped back. "You're never able to do anything right, are you?"

I was shocked. *How dare this child speak to an adult that way?* I didn't say anything more, but I was angry.

We can't have this kind of conflict in our assembly, I thought while driving home that day. *How can God bless unless there is love and respect between the workers?*

After lunch I realized I should pray about the situation. The Lord had a solution, I knew. This talented girl was precious in His sight. The way I handled this situation might make a difference in her life as well as mine.

When I knelt before the Lord, it seemed as if He was saying, "The answer to this situation is for you to humble yourself. Call Chris and talk this over in a Christian way."

So I called Chris that afternoon. "Chris, I don't know why you spoke to me the way you did today. I don't believe the Lord can bless unless you and I can work harmoniously together. So I want you to know that I'm sorry if I've ever hurt or offended you."

"Well, to tell the truth," she answered, "I've always had the feeling that I couldn't play well enough to suit you."

"I'm truly sorry if I've given you that impression, Chris," I said. "I think you play well. I believe the problem lies in getting started. Why don't we try having you give the single starting note loud and clear?"

"All right," Chris said, in a friendlier voice. "And I'm sorry I spoke to you the way I did today."

A warm glow filled my heart as we said good-bye.

Colossians 3:13 says, "Bear with each other and forgive whatever grievances you may have against one another. Forgive as the Lord forgave you."

The Psalmist first exhorted us to live together in harmony in our verse for today. Colossians 3:12–14 tells us how. What wisdom God's Word has for us in regard to human relationships!

Examine your own relationships. Where might they be improved by your using a loving, forgiving, humble approach? Why not begin applying this in whatever relationship problems you're facing?

"If thou wouldst find much favor and peace with God and man,
be very low in thine own eyes. Forgive thyself little
and others much."
—Robert Leighton

❤ Journal Exercise ❤

What troubled relationship are you facing today? How does that disunity make you feel? If you've been focusing only on the other person's role in the difficulty, think about what part you have played. How does God want you to apply Colossians 3:12–14 so that Psalm 133:1 can be a reality in your life? —KCM

Eleven Things To Be Thankful For

Bonnie Watkins

Give thanks to the LORD, for he is good.
His love endures forever.
Psalm 136:1

I found a fat paperback book, *14,000 Things to Be Happy About,* on my desk at school early one morning, a birthday gift from a fellow teacher. When I thumbed through it quickly before the bell rang, I found lists of the things that had made author Barbara Ann Kipfer happy over the years.

I grabbed a pen and spontaneously wrote my own short list. It wasn't too far a stretch from "things to be happy about" to "things to be thankful for." I titled mine "11 Things to Be Thankful For." They were these: homemade corn chowder, puppy breath, wild orchids in Hawaii, sleeping late on Saturday, hazelnut coffee, tickling baby's toes, old hymns of the faith, curling up with a new book, rainy days when you don't have to go anywhere, a sister's love, and that Jesus didn't give up on me.

This five-minute exercise turned into a good morning devotional and cast a rosy glow over the rest of my day. Later, I discovered that after a hard day when I was brain dead, making such a list in my journal was an easy end-of-the-day devotional, too. Besides, seeing the good things in what I had counted a "bad" day helped me to have a new perspective.

Finally, I extended this exercise to my classroom. Each year, the day before Thanksgiving, I read a portion of the book's list; then I show the students some of my list. I try to include something about them, especially the students who don't often excel. For example, "Melinda's smile every day" might be on my list.

I ask them to make a list of their own and to include at least one thing about their parents. After about five minutes, I tell them to stop and count the number of things on their list. If they have seventeen, then their title is "17 Things to Be Thankful For." I ask them to take this list home and give it to their parents the next day.

This exercise works at most grade levels, but it's especially effective in high school because parents no longer see many "papers from school." Each year, several parents thank me for the list they have received. Then I have yet another item to add to my list.

The Psalmist instructs us to be thankful. It's not a suggestion; it's a command. Be thankful! He seems to imply that it's easy to be thankful when we concentrate on God's love and goodness.

Being thankful is a remarkable exercise for our spirits. We exercise our bodies for better health, and this is a way to exercise for better mental and spiritual health.

When we focus on the numerous things that deserve our gratitude, it's easier to overlook the few things we aren't thankful for. What are you thankful for today?

"Let never day nor night unhallow'd pass, But still remember what the Lord hath done."

—William Shakespeare, *Henry VI*, Part 2, Act II, sc. I

❤ Journal Exercise ❤

Do you consider yourself generally thankful or not? If not, why is that? How would other people regard you? Write here as many things as you can that you're grateful for. Give yourself five minutes and amaze yourself at the blessed life you actually have! Then write out a thanksgiving prayer to God. —KCM

First Impression

Ruth Bell Graham

The LORD will fulfill his purpose for me; your love, O LORD, endures forever—do not abandon the works of your hands.
Psalm 138:8

All I saw was a blur. I was on the steps of East Blanchard when a new student passed me. I was going up. He was going down.

He's surely in a hurry, I thought, and went on.

Sunday mornings we had a prayer meeting in Williston lobby before dividing up and going out on gospel team assignments. That morning I heard a new voice pray: strong, clear, urgent.

There is a man who knows to Whom he is speaking, I thought.

I had heard about this new transfer student, who had come from a Bible college in Florida. They said he was a gifted preacher—a young man on whose shoulder God's hand seemed to rest.

Shortly after that, a friend, Johnny Streater, introduced us. Not long after, Bill asked me for our first date—a Sunday afternoon presentation of *The Messiah*.

Now, one does not get to know a person by sitting and listening to a group singing, however inspiring the music. Yet that night I knew he was the one. Someone has said, "Feminine instinct is a great timesaver: it enables a woman to jump at conclusions without bothering with the facts." So I laid it before the Lord and left it there.

❤ *Lesson* ❤

And as they say . . . the rest is history. Ruth and that young, intense, gifted preacher, Billy Graham, dated and then married. Little did Ruth know as she passed that young man in the hall that their lives would forever be entwined for God's glory. A chance meeting, a chance introduction—it would seem—but God had His hand upon those "chances."

He does the same for you and me. Nothing reaches us through God's love filter except that which He intends to use for our good and His glory. His loving intention is to fulfill His every purpose for us and He always intends that purpose for our spiritual benefit. Everything He allows may not seem good from our standpoint, but it is intended for our spiritual growth, that we might become more like Jesus.

Chance meeting? No way! Chance introduction? Not on your life. God's purposes brought Ruth and Billy together and as a result, His loving control was demonstrated. —KCM

"The Spirit's agency is sovereign, like the wind
blowing where it will."
—George Smeaton

❤ Journal Exercise ❤

When you think of God's sovereign love filter wrapped around you, what does it look like in your imagination? Is it wrapped lovingly or thrown around you? Is it whole or does it have holes? What does your picture mean in your understanding of who God is and how He works in your life? Draw a picture here of God's whole love filter carefully wrapped around you. —KCM

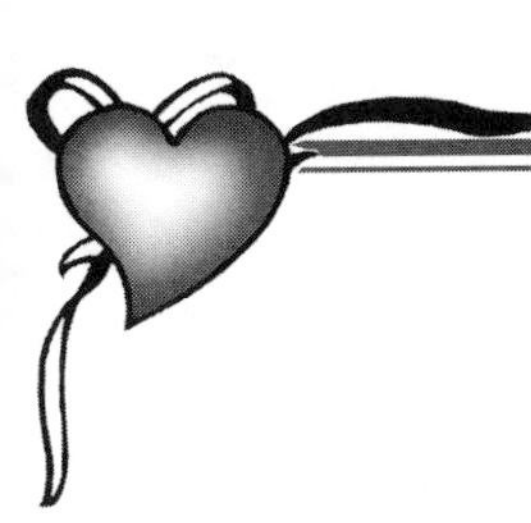
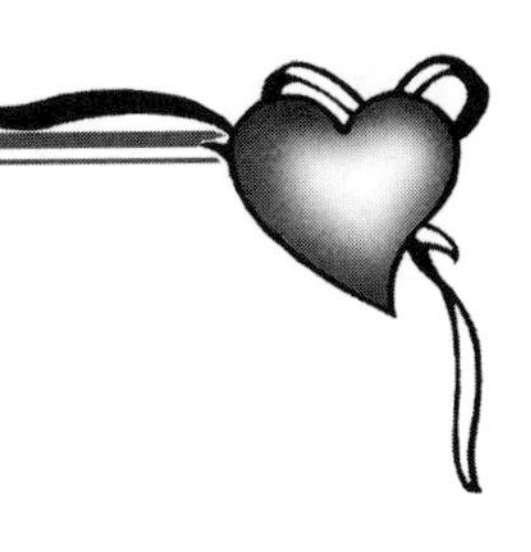

The Invitation

Pamela Rowell

Oh LORD, you have searched me and you know me.
Psalm 139:1

How exciting to be invited to a party! My seven-year-old daughter, JoyAnna, received a birthday invitation in the mail. We read the card together and puzzled over the unfamiliar name of the birthday girl. We looked at the return address for a clue to the sender. No help there. We browsed the school directory and decided we didn't know the girl inviting JoyAnna to her party. After phoning another mother for a description, JoyAnna remembered they had played together on the playground, but didn't know her name. JoyAnna enjoys parties, and decided she would like to go. Thankfully, I hesitated in calling to accept the invitation.

The day before the party, JoyAnna and I had a conversation that troubled my heart.

"Mom, I can go to the party tomorrow. She said I could."

"If she sent you an invitation, she must have wanted you to be there," I assured her.

"She meant to invite JoAnna and not me," she said with her head bowed.

"Oh?" What else could a mother say?

"I told her I would give JoAnna the invitation, but she said JoAnna couldn't come so I could come if I wanted to."

How sad. My heart broke for her. JoyAnna's name is often mis-prounced—pronounced as JoAnna. That wouldn't be a problem except there is a little girl named JoAnna who is also in the second grade and lives in our neighborhood. We thought JoyAnna's special name would set her apart; instead it has caused confusion.

❤ Lesson ❤

I am so glad that God knows each of us by name. Because He created each one of us within His perfect plan and design, He knows each of us as His special child and calls our name, never confusing us with someone else.

Psalm 139:1 rejoices in God's ability to search our hearts and know us. Even though He knows all our imperfections and our struggles, He still chooses to call us His own.

We can rejoice that His invitation is not limited and there is no confusion on His guest list. He is the perfect host. No gift is expected from the guests. He has already provided the greatest gift of all—eternal life—through Jesus' birth and death.

Our perfect Host calls us by name and says, "Come as you are." He sees each of us as an honored guest invited to the most spectacular event of all!

Your name is on the invitation.

Have you given your RSVP?

"A God wise enough to create me and the world I live in is wise enough to watch out for me."
—Philip Yancey

❤ Journal Exercise ❤

How does it make you feel that God has invited you to the most glorious and incredible party of all—eternal life? What do you think that party will be like? What verses can you find in the Bible that describe it? In what ways is your present life like a party? Read John 10:10. Describe how your life is abundant. Then write a prayer of thanksgiving for the blessings of this life and your future home in heaven. —KCM

WEEK TWELVE

God Knows How To Knit

Patti Iverson

For you created my inmost being; you knit me together in my mother's womb. I praise you because I am fearfully and wonderfully made; your works are wonderful, I know that full well.
Psalm 139:13–14

Magic was in the air as children cavorted up and down the grassy hillsides. Our annual Children's Festival was in full swing! Excited preschoolers scampered behind Mother Goose to various booths, animal pens, and storytellers. Older kids lost any sophistication as they tie-dyed brilliantly colored masterpieces, got gooey, clay-gomped hands, and hustled their sweaty bodies on to the next craft booth to concoct treasures 'n treats. Onstage, dancers danced, musicians made music, magicians were mystical.

Thousands of volunteers work all year to create four summer days of fun, intended to charm children and give adults a glimpse of their wonderful past. As the Calligraphy Clown, I sit under a shade tree at the main entrance and write names on tags in a fancy way so we can call each child by name.

A "Queen" strolls through the festivities with her court. What a great privilege it is for the children to be chosen to serve the pretty lady in her cape and crown. It's delightful seeing the boys in their white shirts and the girls gussied up in finery with flowers adorning their hair as they prepare the way for the honored lady.

One evening, as part of the Queen's entourage, two darling sisters in wheelchairs wore tiaras and sashes that proudly proclaimed "Special

Princess." Their limbs were misshapen and flailing, yet they were stunningly beautiful. We chatted as I wrote their names.

"We are having such fun!" said the smaller of the two.

"If you could be any character at the festival, who would you choose to be?" I asked the more outgoing sister.

She replied without a pause, "I love being me and being special. I wouldn't want to ever be anybody else 'cause I am who God made me to be."

They left to continue their quest amid all the other kids running and jumping. I fairly gasped in humility and a sense of being on holy ground. A clown can't cry on the outside, what a mess that would be! But my happy and grateful tears flowed on the inside, in my heart, where it counts.

❤ *Lesson* ❤

So often I fret about both the inside and the outside of the "me" that I am—the way that God made me. Dissatisfaction in how I look, act, and sound compel me to try to be different. Of course, I fail miserably. Yet, I saw the Lord's creative glory in those two most perfect little Princesses at the Children's Festival. They were content with who they were.

Surely, when David wrote his thoughts about how God created him in his mother's womb, he did not feel perfect or complete. Yet, you and I can be grateful for everything we are—fearfully and wonderfully made, hand-knit by God!

"Content thyself with thine estate; neither wish death nor fear . . ."
—Henry Howard

❤ Journal Exercise ❤

If you could tell God anything about how He made you, what would you say to Him? Write it out. Do you think God was smiling or frowning when He designed you? What unkind thing do you say about yourself most often? What is actually the truth about yourself? Memorize Psalm 139:13–14 and repeat it each time you think that "unkind phrase." —KCM

Fingerprints, Faith, And Fresh Water

Janell M. Rardon

My frame was not hidden from you when I was made in the secret place. When I was woven together in the depths of the earth, your eyes saw my unformed body. All the days ordained for me were written in your book before one of them came to be.
Psalm 139:15–16

My little boy and I were running errands together. First on our agenda was the drive-through at the bank.

The clerk's voice came over the intercom. "I'm sorry, Ma'am, you will have to come inside to handle this matter."

With a sigh and a grumble, I parked the car and we went into the bank hand in hand. I waited in line and was finally summoned. The teller instructed me that I had to place my thumbprint on the check I was trying to cash—a new bank policy called "Touchpoint Identification System."

While following her instructions, I reminded my son of the little poem I had taught him, "Starting with Me," by Miss Rosalie Slater in, *Teaching and Learning America's Christian History*:

"God made me special
Like no one else you see;
God made me a witness
To His diversity."

"I remember," he exclaimed, "Everybody in the whole world has different fingerprints! God did that because we are so special."

"That's beautiful," the teller said softly, "Really beautiful."

"And it's absolutely true," I affirmed. "God says we are each fearfully and wonderfully made, and that includes you!" I smiled.

She stopped what she was doing and looked me straight in the eye. "You have no idea what that means to me today," she said. "I really believe God sent you in here today."

I asked her if she had a Bible at home. She nodded, and I encouraged her to look up Psalm 139 before she went to bed. "Locked within this one chapter in the Bible is a special promise for you," I said.

She wrote herself a note about the verse while shaking her head in amazement.

❤ Lesson ❤

Psalm 139:15–16 is a word for all of us. There are times when we all lose sight of who God created us to be. Elohim, our Creator God, knit each of us with tender care and concern with each day of our lives intended to represent Him. Every facet of our hearts, souls, minds, and bodies were fashioned by His loving, caring hands.

God led my son and me into the life of that hurting bank teller. Perhaps God will use you to bring life to someone who is hurting. Using your God-designed uniqueness, pour your living water into a parched soul.

"We are to be centers through which Jesus can flow as rivers of living water in blessing to everyone."
—Oswald Chambers

❤ Journal Exercise ❤

We all have things we don't like about ourselves. Yet God designed each one of us uniquely to represent Him. How does your uniqueness represent Him? Have you cooperated or fought against the "days ordained for" you in God's sovereign plan? Meditate and journal your thoughts on verses like Ephesians 2:10 and 2 Corinthians 5:20. What does God call you and how does that make you feel? —KCM

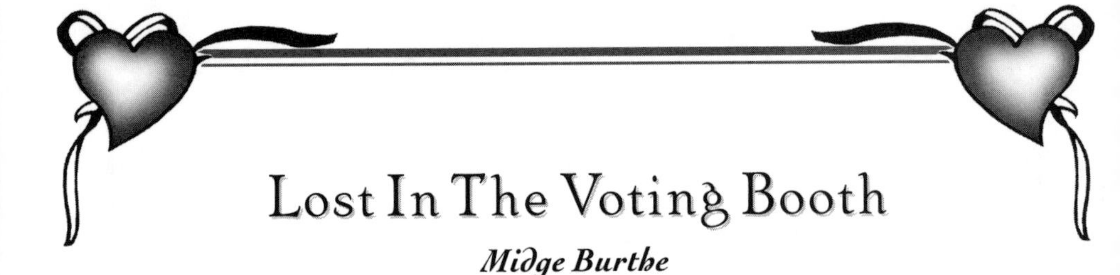

Lost In The Voting Booth

Midge Burthe

How precious to me are your thoughts, O God! How vast is the sum of them! Were I to count them, they would outnumber the grains of sand. When I awake, I am still with You.
Psalm 139:17–18

On the television in our living room, I listened to the presidential candidates debate the issue of trade sanctions for human rights violations. My head swam. The gentleman speaking seemed to disagree with the others, but his words sounded identical to those of the previous speaker. Hoping for clarification, I asked my husband, "Can you tell me what their positions are and how they differ?"

He laughed. "Honey, they don't really have positions. They're just wanting to show they are knowledgeable about the issues without offending anyone and losing votes."

"But how are we supposed to know which one to vote for if we can't understand their positions?" My frustration and confusion surfaced, and I could not keep the irritation out of my voice. I felt naive and more than a little stupid. Suddenly, the men's voices repelled me, and I went to my bedroom.

Bowing my head, I prayed. "Lord, help me to understand. What is Your will in this? Where do I go to educate myself on this election? To whom should I listen? Help me, please. Amen."

For a moment I sat quietly, waiting for God's Word. Then it came. "My thoughts are not the thoughts of this world. Keep your mind on My thoughts. Read and meditate on My Word as you rise and as you lie down to sleep. Never forget that I am Lord and whatever happens is within My will." A great feeling of peace came over me. How wonderful that I have such a Lord! He will never allow me to stray from His will as long as I keep my mind on His thoughts.

❤ Lesson ❤

David was embroiled in political and military turmoil. His kingship was under strong attack from all sides. His every thought must have been stained with the worry of how to outmaneuver his enemies. In his despair, David turned to the Lord and His holy Word, where he found comfort and assurance. The Lord told David to meditate on His Word and to trust Him to take care of everything else.

As David thought of the incredible vastness of God's knowledge, he penned Psalm 139:17–18. He was in awe of a God whose greatness can never be fully understood.

The Lord God's thoughts transported David to a higher place, far from the muck of politics. God's wise mind provides an endless delight of exploration and revelation. In His thoughts we are never confused, never depressed, and never considered stupid, for He welcomes those who recognize their need and seek Him. To cope with the darkness of this world, we have the light of His pure and penetrating truth.

What do you fill your thoughts with? Interest in spiritual things—the thoughts of God? Or fascination with this world? If you choose to seek God, you'll never run out of things to learn about Him.

"I want to know God's thoughts. The rest are details."
—Albert Einstein

❤ Journal Exercise ❤

Are you allowing inappropriate, worldly thoughts to barge in, blocking out the thoughts from God? Are you seeking answers from magazines, newspapers, TV, radio, or the internet rather than voicing them in your prayers? Write your confession to God for looking to the world's ideas and tell Him how you intend to seek His thoughts more often. —KCM

Searching For Holiness

Luis Palau

Search me, O God, and know my heart; test me and know my anxious thoughts. See if there is any offensive way in me, and lead me in the way everlasting.
Psalm 139:23–24

When I was a Bible college student, I did my best to be perfect for God. I read. I studied. I modeled myself after godly men. Then one day in chapel, I finally realized, *It's not me, but God in me, that makes me usable for God. He is the One to search me and lead me in the way I should go.*

King David was not perfect, either. But he longed to be holy. David not only agreed with God about his sins, in his heart he also wanted to agree with God about holiness. In Psalm 139, he says, in effect, "Oh Lord, I hate sin. I hate it in others. I hate it in myself. Teach me, search my motives and my thoughts. Lord, show me what doesn't belong. Show me what makes You sad as You examine my life."

David was a soldier, a general, an ambitious character—but he was also a man with a tender heart who wanted to be holy.

Do you long to be holy? Of course, we all have impure thoughts, and they often attack us when we're least expecting them. We all have moments when our attitudes are ugly and we hate ourselves for it. But the big question is this: Do you *want* to be holy? Do you *want* to be pure? Do you long to be clean? Do you long to be transparent before God and before people?

God—and God alone—can teach us to be holy as He searches our hearts. He will train our spirits to be thirsty for holiness as

David was thirsty for it. As Christians, we are indwelt by God's Holy Spirit. There's no better teacher.

Holiness seems like a distant, impossible goal. God knew it truly was impossible for us, that's why He sent Jesus. As Luis Palau writes, it's not our performance that makes us holy, but Jesus within us. We need not be anxious because God sees our heart. He acknowledges Jesus' robe of righteousness wrapped around us, declaring us "Innocent!" —KCM

"In pursuit of purity of heart, however, we must not fall into another error: the pit of self-condemnation. . . . The time comes when we must forget ourselves and concentrate on Christ, the Word, and the needs of those before us."
—Craig Brian Larson

❤ Journal Exercise ❤

On a scale of one to five (with one being least, and five greatest), what is your desire for holiness? What do you think God would say to you about that? Write it down. What would you say to God about your increased desire for holiness? If there's a lack, ask Him to provide that desire. —KCM

Fright Turned To Might

Dottie G. Bachtell

Praise be to the LORD my Rock, who trains my hands for war, my fingers for battle. He is my loving God and my fortress, my stronghold, and my deliverer, my shield, in whom I take refuge, who subdues peoples under me.
Psalm 144:1–2

My eldest son, Michael, is an Air Force pilot deployed to the Middle East as part of the U.S. peacekeeping forces. During my daily prayer time, I found it difficult to imagine him flying over southern Iraq, patrolling the nighttime skies of the "no-fly zone." Even the name sounded frightful! I prayed, "Oh, Lord, take care of Michael as he flies over—" and then terrible images would appear in my mind, distracting me from my prayer. After a few frightening moments, I would quickly close with, "Lord, keep him safe."

I asked God to help me pray more effectively for Michael, feeling that my attempts were feeble and weak. God led me to some powerful Scriptures on warfare, such as Psalm 144:1–2. I was amazed at the specific references to military matters—things my son faced daily. After reading the verses several times, I inserted Michael's name in my own paraphrased version and came out with the following prayer: "I praise You, Lord, for You are my Rock. You train Michael's hands for war and his fingers for battle. You are Michael's loving God, his fortress, his stronghold, his deliverer and shield. He takes refuge in You, Lord, as You subdue the enemy under him."

My Scripture-filled intercession became bold as I envisioned God training Michael's hands and fingers for the jet's massive control console full of gauges and switches. In my mind's eye, I could see God's mighty defense system, acting like a fortress protecting my son on all sides. I knew God, his great deliverer, was in that single-seat fighter jet right alongside my son, guarding Michael. He was Michael's refuge in the storm and could subdue all enemies below.

❤ *Lesson* ❤

The heavenly Father is so patient. I know He blessed those first prayers, pitiful as they were. He understood the desire of my heart, as well as my difficulty in expressing myself. God led me to use many powerful Scriptures as my guide.

God calls on us to pray for our family and friends, but sometimes we limit our prayers by what our intellect can "see." God's Word changes not only the wording of our prayers, but it can strengthen our underlying faith. As we seek God's direction in intercession and search out applicable promises from God's Word, we begin to "see" beyond our limited vision.

Take a glimpse at God's vast array of spiritual weaponry that battles for us every day, and begin praying past the fences of the natural. View the awesome supernatural power of our limitless heavenly Father.

"The Word of God is the fulcrum upon which the lever of prayer is placed and by which things are mightily moved."
—E. M. Bounds

❤ Journal Exercise ❤

How is praying God's words back to Him superior to prayer based on your own limited wisdom? Write out a Scripture as a prayer for a concern you have right now. You can put in your own name or the name of someone else. Then have the confidence to know God wants to answer your prayer—because it's based on His own desires. —KCM

Biblical Orphans

Jeri Chrysong

The LORD watches over the alien and sustains the fatherless and the widow.
Psalm 146:9a

When I first divorced, I prayed for a father figure for my sons, Lucas and Sammy. I mourned the absence of their father in our home and wanted someone to guide my boys in ways a woman cannot. Although I'm not a widow, my sons are "biblical orphans," because they're growing up without a father. God has promised to sustain the orphans.

I've seen the Lord do that in a variety of creative ways. Doug, one of the men in a Bible study I joined, felt the Lord call him to mentor Luc and Sam. *Finally,* I thought, *my prayers have been answered!*

Doug and the boys have gone camping, fishing, waterskiing, and sometimes just over to Doug's house for a "guys' night." Doug taught Luc how to shave. He also taught my sons the fun of having their unsuspecting mother sit on a whoopee cushion. He has been faithful to his commitment to my boys for many years.

Not only Doug, but also Sunday school teachers, youth workers, and fathers of school chums have befriended Luc and Sammy. Floyd, from my Bible study group, noticed a broken windowpane in my front door, compliments of Sammy, my young pitcher. Floyd came over and, with Sam's "help," repaired the window. *That* was an answer to prayer.

Free car maintenance and repair tips from Tim have been answers to prayer. Dave, a Football Booster Club dad who "adopted" Sammy, dropped by to take him "car shopping" and spent an entire day looking at "really cool cars." Then Dave treated him at a favorite eatery. That was an answer to prayer! Every person who came to watch Luc and Sam play baseball or football, or run track and field, has been an answer to my prayers.

I rejoice when I see how God has sustained us by providing the much-prayed-for role models and father figures. An added benefit for me has been the friendships I've built with the wives of these men.

❤ Lesson ❤

If you find yourself without a parenting partner, trust in your heavenly Father—your parenting partner—to guide you. Psalm 146:9 promises that He will sustain you and your children. Even if you are divorced, He understands that you are without a spouse, and you are included in His definition of "widow." He will provide the wisdom you need as a single parent if you earnestly seek it. He will supply your needs if you depend upon Him.

Your children are fatherless—or motherless—and He wants to meet their needs also. God is your child's heavenly "Daddy," and in Psalm 146:9, He promises to sustain them. He may choose to meet your family's needs through the caring of your church family. Because of that, it's essential that you become involved in a church. Trust that God will prompt caring adults to mentor your child. The unpredictable ways your prayers will be answered will delight you!

"A real friend is one who walks in when the rest
of the world walks out."
—Walter Winchell

❤ Journal Exercise ❤

What are your greatest fears for your children? How has God provided in the past for them? How would you like Him to provide now? Can you surrender those expectations to Him? Can you believe He has a better idea? He loves your children even more than you do. Believe He'll provide what they really need.
—KCM

Credits

"When I Consider Thy Heavens" adapted from *What Works When Life Doesn't* by Stuart Briscoe, Cook Communications Ministries, 1976. Copied with permission. May not be further reproduced. All rights reserved. [8]

"A Lesson from the Tax Man" from *Falling into Greatness* by Lloyd John Ogilvie, Thomas Nelson Publishers, Nashville, TN, 1984. [11]

"What Are You Haunted By?" from *My Utmost for His Highest* by Oswald Chambers, Barbour and Company, Inc., Uhrichsville, OH, 1935. [35]

"Waiting, Waiting, Waiting . . ." from *He's Gonna Toot And I'm Gonna Scoot* by Barbara Johnson, Word, Nashville, TN, 1999. Used by permission of the author. [41]

"When An Answer to Prayer Is Delayed" from *What Happens When God Answers* by Evelyn Christenson, Word Books, Waco, TX, 1986. Used by permission. All rights reserved. [44]

"Sheltered" adapted from *It's About Home* by Patsy Clairmont, Servant Publications, Ann Arbor, MI, 1998. Used with permission. [56]

"Don't Make It Worse" adapted from *Tough Times Never Last, but Tough People Do!* by Robert H. Schuller, Thomas Nelson, Nashville, TN, 1983. [77]

"Anywhere But Germany" from *Not I, But Christ* by Corrie ten Boom, Thomas Nelson, Nashville, TN, 1983. [80]

"The Power Of Forgiveness" from *Just Like Jesus* by Max Lucado, Word, Nashville, TN, 1998. Used by permission. All rights reserved. [107]

"The End of All Sorrow" from *Surprised by Suffering* by R.C. Sproul, Tyndale House Publishing, Wheaton, IL, 1989. [143]

"Facing Death" from *Hope for the Troubled Heart* by Billy Graham, Word Books, Dallas, TX: 1991. Used by permission. All rights reserved. [146]

"An Encouraging Word" from *A Touch of His Peace* by Charles Stanley, Zondervan Publishing House, Grand Rapids, MI, 1993. Used by permission of Zondervan Publishing House. [161]

"Laugh Again!" from *Laugh Again* by Charles R. Swindoll, Word Books, Dallas, TX, 1991. Used by permission. All rights reserved. [170]

"First Impression" from *It's My Turn* by Ruth Bell Graham, Fleming H. Revell, Old Tappan, NJ, 1982. [194]

"Starting with Me" (poem) from *Teaching and Learning America's Christian History* developed by Rosalie Slater, published by the Foundation for American Christian Education, San Francisco, CA, 1965. Used by permission. [203]

Contributors

Anita J. Anderson is a freelance writer and a homemaker for a spouse who travels much on business. She has four grandchildren and experience in nursing, counseling, gardening, and travel, including foreign missions. Contact: 9936 W. Moccasin Trail, Wexford, PA 15090-9309. (724) 935-5647. glaaja@usaor.net. [86]

Candy Neely Arrington has just completed her first novel and enjoys writing poetry and devotionals. She and her husband and two children live in Spartanburg, South Carolina, where she is a real estate broker and youth discipleship leader. Contact: CNAnSptbg@aol.com or icanwrite2@juno.com. [29]

Dottie G. Bachtell is a wife, mom, and Industrial Chaplain with Marketplace Ministries. She loves to write poetry, devotionals, articles, and stories about her family. She especially enjoys her Sunday school class, Christian critique group, and Bible study fellowship. Contact: Chuckdot@worldnet.att.net. [212]

Heather Harlan Bacus is a professional singer, songwriter, storyteller, and speaker. She is founder of her own company, Looking Up Productions. She has one recording project for children, *I Want More Balloons*. Contact: 1005 W. Lafayette, Jacksonville, IL 62650. (217) 243-4585. bacuslup@csj.net. [185]

Vivian Lee Baniak is a freelance writer, trainer for Personality Plus, and Precept Bible study leader. She speaks at women's events and homeschool groups on the topics of personality, personal finances, and principles for living from God's Word. Contact: (909) 476-3930. mmviviandy@iol7.com. [158]

Kelly Bell is a pastor's wife, director of Women's Ministry, and mother of two. She enjoys teaching and speaking to women's groups, along with writing Bible studies and devotionals for women. Contact: 24225 Monroe, Murrieta, CA 92562. (909) 677-5667. kbell@ccmurrieta.com. [182]

Steven S. Bovia is active in the Epicopal church as a lay reader and adult Bible study teacher. He has done work toward a Master of Divinity degree at Ashland Theological Seminary. He writes for www.Jonahsway.com. Contact: 37 Townsend St., Greenwich, OH 44837. (419) 752-6150. email@Jonahsway.com. [113]

Rose Brandon is a writer and speaker living in Sault Ste. Marie, Canada. She and husband Doug have three children and are active in their church and community. Rose's articles, short stories, and devotionals have been published in many Christian magazines. [137]

Charles R. Brown has worked as a radio announcer, custodian, teacher, and clown. Currently he's in the title industry. He has done stand-up comedy, and in 1999 got his first senior meal. He and wife, Bobbie, have four children and three grandchildren. [176]

Elsie H. Brunk is a wife, mother of four, and grandmother of ten. She is a freelance writer with articles and devotionals in a number of publications. Contact: 5004 Turners Mill Ln., Harrisonburg, VA 22802. (540) 833-6590. ebrunk@gateway.net. [98]

Midge Burthe is a retired naval officer with a master's degree in psychology. She lives with her husband and two youngest children. Contact: 38332 Mira Monte Ave., Palmdale, CA 93551. (661) 267-0480. burthe@earthlink.net. [206]

Jeri Chrysong, poet/humorist, resides in Huntington Beach, California, with sons, Luc and Sam, and pugs, Puddy and Mabel. Her work has been featured in other Starburst books and periodicals. Hobbies are writing, photography, and watching her kids play sports. [215]

Joan Clayton and her husband, Emmitt, are retired educators. They reside in Portales, New Mexico. They each have thirty-one years of service with the public schools. They have three sons and six grandchildren. Contact: joan@yucca.net. [122]

Jan Coleman's writing has appeared in dozens of national magazines and anthologies including the Chicken Soup series. After she was single-again for twelve years, God finally brought Carl, who was worth the wait. Contact: 2050 Canal Street, Auburn, CA 95603. jwriter@foothill.net. [179]

Heather Collard is an elementary substitute teacher. She enjoys playing the piano, and is currently involved in her church's letter writing ministry, as well as the drama ministry at a friend's church. Contact: 2149 McCormack Ln., Placentia, CA 92870. (714) 528-9637. [47]

Maria Conklin lives in Kendall Park, New Jersey, with her husband, Willie, and daughters Jennifer and Emily. Maria and Willie teach a family-and-marriage Sunday school class at their church. Contact: mcspeaks@optonline.net. [23]

Barbara Curtis is mother to eleven, grandmother to five. She is the author *of Small Beginnings, Ready, Set, Read!* along with four hundred articles in more than forty magazines, including *Guideposts, Christian Parenting Today, Focus on the Family,* and *World*. Contact: www.barbaracurtis.com. [38]

Karen Davis, creator of the play "Chronicles of a Liberated Woman" is a corporate trainer, speaker, and writer. She and her husband conduct seminars on the critical importance of renewing the mind. Contact: PO Box 3000-469, Chino, CA 91708. (909) 988-6067. kard@gte.net. [155]

Gayle DeSalles is an author and Precept Bible study leader. Her passion is communicating fundamental truths about God's character through storytelling. She's a secretary for a private university in

Nashville and enjoys reading and the outdoors. Contact: 123 Cedarwood Lane, Madison, TN 37115-2765. Gaylewrites@aol.com. [53]

Pat Devine is an author, poet, and memoirist. She delights in husband, grandchildren, travel, and leading workshops to encourage others to explore their faith through journal writing. Contact: 419 Argent Ave., Ferguson, MO 63135-2205. (314) 521-0419. patdevine@excelonline.com. [131]

Pamela F. Dowd is a freelance writer for various publications and for DaySpring and Celebration Greetings. You'll find more of her short stories in *Why Fret That God Stuff?, Seasons of a Woman's Heart,* and *Heart-Stirring Stories of Romance*. Contact: dowpub@juno.com. [71]

Laura DuBell Drewer is a reading specialist and has created learning games. She writes devotionals and a newspaper column, "Parents as Teachers." She and William, a former pastor, have six children and nine grandchildren. Contact: 1221E Lakeshore Drive West, Shelton, WA 98584. (306) 427-8717. Drewersr@juno.com. [20]

Les Enloe teaches junior high Bible and math. Spending time with his family is his favorite pastime. When he's not doing that, he enjoys reading the Bible and writing. Contact: lenloe@msn.com. [173]

Judy Gale is a pastor's wife, homemaker, mother of three, grandmother to seven, avid reader, fledgling writer, and encourager in the body of Christ. Contact: 395 Duane Street, Glen Ellyn, IL 60137. (630) 858-3844. [32]

Ida Rose Heckard writes and speaks on inspirational and educational topics. Her articles have appeared in *Today's Christian Woman, Excellence*, and *Christian Home and School*. Educators, homeschoolers, and women's groups enjoy her presentations. Contact: (808) 877-5251. Live4Him80@aol.com; http://hometown.aol.com/live4him80/page/index.htm. [62]

Elizabeth Hey is a freelance writer and a member of Kansas City Christian Writer's Network. She and her husband home educate their three children, ages twelve, nine, and six. [164]

Sheila S. Hudson, Bright Ideas founder, is a freelance writer and speaker. Credits include *Chocolates for a Woman's Heart, God's Vitamin "C" for the Spirit of Men, Taking Education Higher, Chocolates for a Young Woman's Heart,* and *Chocolates for a Woman's Blessing*. Contact: (706) 546-5085. sheila@naccm.org. [65]

Patti Iverson's passions include Christ, her Fire Chief husband, clowning, cuddling sick babies weekly at the hospital, coordinating volunteers for Campus Life, and cooking. She is capable with a capacious heart! Contact: 1224 N. Modoc Unit 24, Medford, OR, 97504. randpi@cdsnet.net. [200]

Brenda Jank loves snowy winter hikes, sunrise devotions, and children. With her family of six, she lives, works, and ministers at a Christian Retreat Center in NE Indiana. As the Lord allows, Brenda writes, speaks, and leads retreats. Contact: 1596 S. 150 W. Albion, IN, 46701. (219) 636-7095. bjank1@juno.com. [101]

Laurie D. Jenkins is a wife and mother of two school-aged children. She enjoys spending time with her family and is involved with women's and children's ministries. Contact: 1568 NE Hyde St., Hillsboro, OR, 97124. (503) 640-9343. LaurieJ1961@cs.com. [74]

Gail Black Kopf, a freelance writer, is the author of *Rubicon* (Thomas Nelson) and has twice won Greater Philadelphia Christian Writer's Contest. A seasoned writer who has numerous publishing credits, she currently resides in Summersville, West Virginia. Contact: gbkinspire@mtec.net. [119]

Marilyn Krebs and her husband are retired pastors. She writes monthly for a senior newspaper and is editor of a newsletter for retired pastors. Her articles have appeared in *Clarity, Pentecostal*

Evangel, *Woman Alive!*, and devotional books. Contact: (864) 296-3732. pkrebs1@juno.com. [149]

Ileana Landon owns a marketing/public relations company in Ontario, California, and lives with her husband, Mark, and their two boys, Michael and Eric. Her dream is to continue writing inspirational books for women and children. Contact: ileana@landonagency.com. [26]

Dr. Muriel Larson has had seventeen books and thousands of writings and songs published. She is a counselor, musician, and public speaker, and has taught at various writers conferences. Contact: 10 Vanderbilt Circle, Greenville, SC 29609-4009. (864) 244-4993. MKLJOY@aol.com. [188]

Jane E. Maxwell is a retired RN, mother of four children and grandmother of two. She enjoys writing inspirational and health articles, devotionals, and essays. Involved in church, Jane also spends time in hospice ministry and with single mothers, along with prevention of domestic violence. Contact: 1704 Pearl St., Vestal, NY 13850. [134]

Cindi McMenamin, a pastor's wife, mother, and national speaker, is the author of *Heart Hunger: Letting God Meet Your Emotional Needs*. She serves as co-director of women at Valley Bible Church in San Marcos, California. Contact: 408 W. San Marcos Blvd. #116, San Marcos, CA 92069. cindispeaks@msn.com. [110]

Kathy Collard Miller has authored forty books including *Through His Eyes* and *Why Do I Put So Much Pressure on Myself?* She speaks nationally and internationally about spiritual growth and relationships. Contact: PO Box 1058, Placentia, CA. 92871. (714) 993-2654. www.larryandkathy.com. [17, 125]

DiAnn Mills is a wife and mother of four adult sons and author of short stories, articles, devotions, a novella, and three novels.

Contact: 14410 Dracaena Court, Houston, TX 77070. millsdg@flash.net; www.rehobothministries.com. [14]

Penny Schlaf Musco is a homemaker and freelance writer in New Jersey who doesn't go in the water much anymore because she'd rather sit under an umbrella at the beach and read. Contact: pmusco@viconet.com. [104]

Mary Beth Nelson is a published freelance writer who lives with her husband. She writes inspirational articles, devotionals, poetry, music, children's writings, book reviews, and journalistic writings. Contact: Box 326, Clarendon, TX 79226. (806) 874-2532. [128]

Sharon Norris is a dynamic, gifted communicator whose heartfelt, biblically sound messages encourage audiences to be "real" in and about faith. Contact: PO Box 1519, Inglewood, CA 90308. SajWriter@aol.com. [152]

Luis Palau is an internationally renowned evangelist and author of more than forty books, including *Where Is God When Bad Things Happen?* (Doubleday) and *A Man after God's Heart* (Discovery House Publishers). Contact: P.O. Box 1173, Portland, OR 97207. lpea@palau.org; www.lpea.org. [209]

Sheila Rabe is a popular writer and speaker. Her books, *I Hate Whining Except When I'm Doing It* and *It's a Wonderful Midlife,* published by Christian Publications, are available through most bookstores. Contact: www.sheilasplace.com. [68]

Janell M. Rardon, wife and homeschooling mom of three, is a Christian communicator and educator whose passion is to see the family unit thrive. She also speaks. Contact: rardon@edifax.com. [203]

Pamela Rowell enjoys being a wife and mother. An avid reader, she feels God leading her to write. She coordinates special events for her church's women's ministry and speaks on spiritual gifts. Contact: 38 Covington, Longview, TX. pamela@rowell.ourfamily.com. [197]

David Sanford is Vice President of Publishing and Internet Ministries for the Luis Palau Evangelistic Association and coauthor (with his wife, Renee) of the "Living Faith Bible" (Tyndale House Publishers). Contact: 6406 N.E. Pacific St., Portland, OR 97213. d_sanford@palau.org. [2]

Doris Schuchard is a wife and mother of two teenagers. She enjoys writing children's stories and adult devotionals. Her hobbies include traveling, making crafts, reading, and watching for the surprise gifts—big and small—God blesses her with. [89]

Nanette Thorsen-Snipes has published more than three hundred fifty articles, columns, devotions, and reprints in publications such as Honor Books, Broadman and Holman, *Parenting Today's Teen*, *Breakaway*, and *Home Life*. Contact: P. O. Box 1596, Buford, GA 30515. (770) 945-3093. jsnipes212@aol.com. [83]

Maureen Stirsman is passionate about her husband and their children, Thomas and Susan. Her grandson, Matthew, puts the spin in her world. She is currently writing a book of stories about members of her Sunday school class. Contact: 965 Horizon Pky., Buford, GA. 30518. tstirs@freewwweb.com. [59]

Tim Thomas resides in Jefferson, Georgia, with his wife, Leigh Ann, and their children, Sam and Hannah. Mr. Thomas is a reporter for *The Jackson Herald*. Contact: (706) 367-2348. SpeckCh@aol.com. [5]

Bonnie Watkins is thankful for her husband and two collegiate sons. She teaches at Hyde Park Baptist High School. She is director of Austin Christian Writers' Guild. Contact: 10102 Chukar Circle, Austin, TX 78758-5530. (512) 837-7094. dwatkins@austin.cc.tx.us. [191]

C. Ellen Watts writes regularly for Christian and inspirational markets. This homemaker and author of five books, mom to five daughters, grandma to sixteen, and great-grandmother to two likes to mentor young writers. Contact: 702 Alderwood Ln., Nampa, ID 83651-2477. (208) 466-0813. [116]

Ted Weaver, husband, father, freelance writer, speaker, and teacher writes under the name TEDBITS to describe the many funny and often embarrassing events of his life. Contact: 310 Sedona Drive, Colorado Springs, CO 80921. (719) 487-0395. TEDBITS@Juno.com. [92]

Christa Weisser is a ministry assistant to a pastor at Palm Beach Gardens Christ Fellowship. She works with senior high youth and young adults. Contact: 5312 Northlake Blvd., Palm Beach Gardens, FL 33418. cgweisse77@aol.com. [167]

Debbie Wong is a speaker, singer, and author. By interweaving songs with practical, biblical advice, she encourages women to start dreaming again and to discover the full life God offers. Contact: PO Box 1391, Monrovia, CA. 91017. (626) 303-0558. heartsdesire@mail.com; http://turn.to/heartsdesire. [140]

Ginny Yttrup is passionate about her relationship with Christ and sharing the message of His redemptive love. She's also passionate about her husband, Kevin, and their two sons. Contact: 4645 Hidden Oaks Lane, Loomis, CA 95650. (916) 660-0195. [95]

POPULAR BOOKS BY STARBURST PUBLISHERS®

An Expressive Heart: Stories, Lessons, and Exercises Inspired by the Psalms
Edited by Kathy Collard Miller
An intimate book of inspirational lessons from the best-selling editor of the *God's Abundance* collection. Each selection includes a passage from the poetic Book of Psalms, an inspirational story, lesson, quotation, and idea for personal journaling with room to write. The Psalms provide an unmatched guide for anyone who wants to know God better, and *An Expressive Heart* will help you say what's on your heart.
(trade paper) ISBN 1892016508 **$12.99**

Bible Seeds: A Simple Study-Devotional for Growing in God's Word
From the creators of the God's Word for the Biblically-Inept™ series
Growing your faith is like tending a garden—just plant the seed of God's Word in your heart, tend it with prayer, and watch it blossom. At the heart of this unique study is a Bible verse or "seed" that is combined with an inspirational lesson, a word study, application tips, thought questions with room to write, a prayer starter, and a final thought.
(trade paper) ISBN 1892016443 **$13.99**

God Things Come in Small Packages: Celebrating the Little Things in Life
By Susan Duke, LeAnn Weiss, Caron Loveless, and Judith Carden
Enjoy touching reminders of God's simple yet generous gifts to brighten our days and gladden our hearts! Treasures like a sunset over a vast, sparkling ocean; a child's trust; or the crystalline dew on a spider's web come to life in this elegant compilation. Such occasions should be celebrated as if gift wrapped from God; they're his hallmarks! Personalized Scripture is artfully combined with compelling stories and reflections.
(cloth) ISBN 1892016281 **$12.95**

God Things Come in Small Packages for Moms: Rejoicing in the Simple Pleasures of Motherhood
By Susan Duke, LeAnn Weiss, Caron Loveless, and Judith Carden
The "small" treasures God plants in a mom's day shine in this delightful book. Savor priceless stories, which encourage you to value treasures like a shapeless, ceramic bowl presented with a toothy grin; a child's hand clinging to yours on a crowded bus; or a handful of wild-

flowers presented on a hectic day. Each story combines personalized Scripture with heart-warming vignettes and inspiring reflections.
(cloth) ISBN 189201629X **$12.95**

Women of the Bible—God's Word for the Biblically-Inept™

By Kathy Collard Miller

Finally, a Bible perspective just for women! Gain valuable insight from the successes and struggles of such women as Eve, Esther, Mary, Sarah, and Rebekah. Interesting icons like "Get Close to God," "Build Your Spirit," and "Grow Your Marriage" will make it easy to incorporate God's Word into your daily life.
(trade paper) ISBN 0914984063 **$16.95**

• Learn more at www.biblicallyinept.com •

What's in the Bible for . . .™ Women

By Georgia Curtis Ling

What does the Bible have to say to women? Women of all ages will find biblical insight on topics that are meaningful to them in four sections: Wisdom for the Journey; Family Ties; Bread, Breadwinners, and Bread Makers; and Fellowship and Community Involvement. This book uses illustrations, bullet points, chapter summaries, and icons to make understanding God's Word easier than ever!
(trade paper) ISBN 1892016109 **$16.95**

What's in the Bible for . . .™ Mothers

By Judy Bodmer

Is home schooling a good idea? Is it okay to work? At what age should I start treating my children like responsible adults? What is the most important thing I can teach my children? If you are asking these questions and need help answering them, *What's in the Bible for . . . Mothers* is especially for you! Simple and user-friendly, this motherhood manual offers hope and instruction for today's mothers by jumping into the lives of mothers in the Bible (e.g., Naomi, Elizabeth, and Mary) and by exploring biblical principles that are essential to being a nurturing mother.
(trade paper) ISBN 1892016265 **$16.95**

Seasons of a Woman's Heart: A Daybook of Stories and Inspiration

Edited by Lynn D. Morrissey

A woman's heart is complex. This daybook of stories, quotes, Scriptures, and daily reflections will inspire and refresh. Christian women share their heartfelt thoughts on Seasons of Faith, Growth, Guidance, Nurturing, and Victory. Includes Christian writers Kay Arthur, Emilie Barnes, Luci Swindoll, Jill Briscoe, and Florence Littauer.
(cloth) ISBN 1892016036 **$18.95**

Treasures of a Woman's Heart: A Daybook of Stories and Inspiration
Edited by Lynn D. Morrissey
Join the best-selling editor of *Seasons of a Woman's Heart* in this touching sequel where she unlocks the treasures of women and glorifies God with Scripture, reflection, and a compilation of stories. Explore heartfelt living with vignettes by Kay Arthur, Elisabeth Elliot, Emilie Barnes, Claire Cloninger, and more.
(cloth) ISBN 1892016257 **$18.95**

Purchasing Information

www.starburstpublishers.com

Books are available from your favorite bookstore, either from current stock or special order. To assist bookstores in locating your selection, be sure to give title, author, and ISBN. If unable to purchase from a bookstore, you may order direct from STARBURST PUBLISHERS. When ordering please enclose full payment plus shipping and handling as follows:

Post Office (4th class)
$4.00 with purchase of up to $20.00
$5.00 ($20.01–$50.00)
9% of purchase price for purchases of $50.01 and up

Canada
$5.00 (up to $35.00)
15% ($35.01 and up)

United Parcel Service (UPS)
$5.00 (up to $20.00)
$7.00 ($20.01–$50.00)
12% ($50.01 and up)

Overseas
$5.00 (up to $25.00)
20% ($25.01 and up)

Payment in U.S. funds only. Please allow two to four weeks minimum for delivery by USPS (longer for overseas and Canada). Allow two to seven working days for delivery by UPS. Make checks payable to and mail to:

Starburst Publishers®
P.O. Box 4123
Lancaster, PA 17604

Credit card orders may be placed by calling 1-800-441-1456, Mon.–Fri., 8:30 A.M. to 5:30 P.M. Eastern Standard Time. Prices are subject to change without notice. Catalogs are available for a 9 x 12 self-addressed envelope with four first-class stamps.